Praise for *Sun Tzu: Strategies for Marketing*

"A unique combination of ancient wisdom and real-world experience."

Carl Glass, Sr. VP, Operations
Varsity Brands, Inc.

"Deceptively simple in execution but powerful in content. The serious executive will find the core concepts to be among the most profound lessons to be found anywhere in marketing literature."

Kathleen Newton, Publisher
Oregon Coast Newspapers

"This book offers excellent resources to corporate CEOs to broaden their visions and enrich strategies for success."

Zhai Zhihai, Fellow
International Strategic Studies
Peoples Republic of China

"This is the book that will make you an effective and efficient leader."

Jere Calmes, Editorial Director
Entrepreneur Press

"Exploits the flexible timelessness of Sun Tzu, reworks it, and adds more wisdom. The result, a marketing book par excellence. Digest this book and your purse will never be empty."

Jusuf Hariman, Ph.D.
Writing Fellow, Manuscript Assessor
Fellowship of Australian Writers

D1298690

SUN TZU

Strategies
for Marketing

12 Essential Principles
for Winning the War for Customers

Gerald A. Michaelson

with

Steven W. Michaelson

BOWLING GREEN STATE UNIVERSITY
DISCARDED
LIBRARY

McGraw-Hill

New York   Chicago   San Francisco   Lisbon   London
Madrid   Mexico City   Milan   New Delhi   San Juan
Seoul   Singapore   Sydney   Toronto

BOWLING GREEN STATE
UNIVERSITY LIBRARIES

The McGraw·Hill Companies

McGraw-Hill A Division of The McGraw-Hill Companies Copyright ©2004 by Gerald A. Michaelson. All rights reserved. Printed in the United States of America. Except as permitted under the United States Copyright Act of 1976, no part of this publication may be reproduced or distributed in any form or by any means, or stored in a data base or retrieval system, without the prior written permission of the publisher.

1 2 3 4 5 6 7 8 9 0   AGM/AGM   0 9 8 7 6 5 4 3

ISBN 0-07-142731-7

Translations from the Chinese by Pan Jiabin, Liu Ruxian, and A. L. Sadler.

McGraw-Hill books are available at special quantity discounts to use as premiums and sales promotions, or for use in corporate training programs. For more information, please write to the Director of Special Sales, Professional Publishing, McGraw-Hill, Two Penn Plaza, New York, NY 10121-2298. Or contact your local bookstore.

Library of Congress Cataloging-in-Publication Data

Michaelson, Gerald A.
   Sun Tzu strategies for marketing : 12 essential
principles for winning the war for customers / by Gerald A.
Michaelson. — 1st ed.
         p. cm.
   ISBN 0-07-142731-7 (alk. paper)
1. Marketing. 2. Sunzi, 6th cent. B.C. Sunzi bing fa. I. Title.
   HF5415.M5268 2004
   658.8'001—dc22

                                        2003018815

 This book is printed on recycled, acid-free paper containing a minimum of 50% recycled de-inked fiber.

*This book is dedicated with love
to our favorite customers,
Jan and Sue Michaelson*

CONTENTS

CONTENTS

Preface

War is a matter of vital importance to the state;
a matter of life and death, the road either to survival or to ruin.
Hence, it is imperative that it be thoroughly studied.

Sun Tzu
The Art of War

Why is a book written 500 years before the birth of Christ a modern-day best-seller? Why do coaches, professors, and business executives read Sun Tzu's *The Art of War*? Why does HBO's Tony Soprano quote the Master's work? What are the marketing applications of the timeless wisdom found in this ancient classic?

The Art of War is recognized as the concentrated essence of winning strategy. Within Sun Tzu's principles are the foundations for understanding the strategic principles of modern marketing. Gaining one insight will lead you to want to find more.

The Art of War is the cornerstone of Eastern military and business strategy. Today, there are more than a dozen translations of this ancient work into the English language. Dozens more apply the translations to business, sports, and personal success. Copies of *The Art of War* can be found in almost every language.

The basic tenet of Sun Tzu's philosophy is that if your strategy is well founded, you will win—and if you have a truly great strategy, you will win without fighting. This Eastern emphasis on overcoming your opponent with strategic wisdom differs significantly from Western strategy, which emphasizes action (fighting the big battle) as the way to win.

The strength of *The Art of War* for the contemporary manager is its simplicity. Inscribing laboriously on bamboo strips, Sun Tzu had to make every thought meaningful. There was nothing very complicated about battle in Sun Tzu's time. When battle was required, the war was won by foreknowledge, calculation, deception, and maneuver. It is the very simplicity of the ancient battle strategies that helps in making the transition from yesterday's lessons to tomorrow's plans.

Sun Tzu's maxims are simple, yet profound; brief, yet deep. The power of these concepts is overwhelming. They apply equally well to business and to everyday life. To win, we need Sun Tzu's power of the extraordinary applied in a precisely timed stroke to develop a torrent of momentum. Ask any Olympic champion about the momentum of extraordinary effort at just the right moment.

Several unique benefits accrue to the reader as a result of the unique organization and content of this book.

1. The 12 principles of marketing strategy are the outline for applying Sun Tzu's wisdom to marketing. We cannot be certain that the translations maintain the flow of the original text; some points seem to belong in other chapters. By extracting the significant passages that apply to business and organizing them within the principles of marketing strategy it is now easier for the reader to understand and apply this timeless wisdom.

2. To give the reader a more thorough insight into the value of Eastern strategic thought, we have included wisdom from Sun Tzu's ancient contemporaries. The most significant of these excerpts are from the seldom published "Wu Chi on *The Art of War*" and "The Precepts of Ssu Ma Jang Chu." Their comments will aid in understanding and applying the ancient strategies.

3. This work uniquely combines both Eastern and Western thought. Including the wisdom of Western military commanders aids in getting ideas to apply in the everyday combat (tactics) of marketing.

PREFACE

We present this work not with the belief that business is war, but rather that we can find useful business applications in a study of military strategy. The wisdom of the ancient Chinese was more about how to avoid war (strategy) than to fight a war.

It takes study to really understand the lessons of Sun Tzu. Reading the book only once is like attempting to learn karate by watching an expert chop a plank in a single blow. With this single lesson, one knows only what to do, not how to do it. To be an expert, one must first be a student.

Your success in applying this ancient wisdom is our success. Our every wish is for your continued success.

Gerald A. Michaelson
Steven W. Michaelson

www.TeamMichaelson.com
E-mail: SunTzu@TeamMichaelson.com

Introduction

The Principles
of Marketing Strategy

Over thousands of years, principles have been developed that serve as guidelines governing action. Sun Tzu lists five conditions and seven attributes as prerequisites for laying plans. Marketing's original four Ps have been expanded to eight. The American army field manual lists nine principles as the foundation of its strategies. From the armies of the world and from practical experience, we have distilled 12 principles as the cornerstone of great marketing.

All principles embody these characteristics:

- Laws indicating the wisdom of certain actions
- Conditions that can lead to success
- Fundamental truths relevant to the success of the discipline

Following the principles does not guarantee victory. Ignore the principles, and you will surely lose. Perhaps a principle is most of all a guide that can sometimes be violated, but must always be considered. Principles are most often ignored by young nations and young companies. Substantial hard evidence indicates that winners adhere to principles.

Principles do not change over time. As we shall see in applying the timeless wisdom of Sun Tzu, the same basic principles have directed great leaders for centuries. Tactical doctrine is revised with every change in technology or technique.

In advice for applying principles, military strategist Edward Luttwak writes:

> Some writers attempting to use the military as a basis for business lessons have ignored the principles. No doubt, they found them frustratingly vague. But it is precisely the principles of war that best capture the essential lessons of the military experience, as opposed to mere techniques, which seem more useful at first because they can be precise, but which also turn out to be inapplicable to real-life needs in most cases.

It would be folly to believe that all principles apply in all situations. You should violate the principles only when you truly know that you are violating them. To know the principles and violate them is to take risks. The further you stray from the principles, the greater the risk. Professionals understand the subtleties of the principles; amateurs ignore the principles. Both take risks. Both win and lose. Only one has the odds in his or her favor. Only in unusual circumstances do great military and marketing generals take the risk of violating principles. Amateurs violate principles simply because others have violated them.

Principles adapted from war are a foundation for sales and marketing strategies. We shall consider these principles as a foundation for the "soft science" of marketing, where formulas are based on probabilities rather than certainties.

The application of these principles is an art. It is in this art that judgment comes into play. Application requires good judgment based on an understanding of the principles. The application to the planning function is called strategy. Their application to the execution of the plan is tactics.

Analyze the principles thoroughly. The assessment before the battle is often ignored in the rush to action.

First Principle: Honor the Customer
If the customer purchase your product or service, nothing else matters.

Second Principle: Organization of Intelligence
Know your market as well as you know yourself.

Third Principle: Maintenance of the Objective
A clear intention and a steady aim.

Fourth Principle: A Secure Position
Occupy a position that cannot easily be taken by your opponents.

Fifth Principle: Offensive Action
Keep on the offensive to secure freedom of action.

Sixth Principle: Surprise

Surprise is the best way to gain psychological dominance and deny the initiative to your opponent.

Seventh Principle: Maneuver

The easiest routes are often the most heavily defended; the longest way round can be the shortest way home.

Eighth Principle: Concentration of Resources

Mass sufficiently superior force at the decisive place and time.

Ninth Principle: Economy of Force

Assess accurately where you employ your resources.

Tenth Principle: Command Structure

The management process unleashes the power of human resources.

Eleventh Principle: Personal Leadership

It requires the leader's faith in his or her people and their faith in the leader's ability to win.

Twelfth Principle: Simplicity

Even the simplest plans are difficult to execute.

First Principle
Honor the Customer

Because the customer has a need, we have a job to do.
Because the customer has a choice, we must be
the better choice.
Because the customer has sensibilities, we must
be considerate.

Because the customer has an urgency, we must be quick.
Because the customer is unique, we must be flexible.
Because the customer has high expectations,
we must excel.

Because the customer has influence, we have hope of
more customers.
Because of the customer, we exist.

—Anon

> *STRATEGICALLY*
> Honoring the customer aims at building
> a lifelong relationship.
>
> *TACTICALLY*
> Honoring the customer aims at satisfaction
> with every interaction.

If the customer doesn't purchase your product or service, nothing else matters.

 Sun Tzu's "customers" were the people—the citizens of the empire. In marketing, people are our customers, and our customers are king—we serve at their pleasure.

SERVE YOUR CUSTOMERS

Every aspect of marketing must focus on the customer. He or she is the judge and jury of your marketing and your business.

The ultimate objective of marketing is to produce products and services that not only satisfy customers' needs but delight them, so they will return and buy again. Marketing is all about winning and retaining customers. Use the customer as a compass to determine the direction of your marketing programs. Customer feedback tells where you should be going. If you do not have marketing data to guide your business, at the end of the day you will not have a business.

So we need to concern ourselves first with the principle "Honor the Customer." To serve our customers, we need to

- Know who they are
- Know what they want
- And give them what they want

We serve our customers by giving them what they want, when they want it, better than anyone else. Let's be clear:

- Not everyone is a potential customer. The breadth of our products and services determines which people are our customers. Equally important, we are, in effect, declaring which people are not our customers.
- We determine how we will serve customers. We meet them at the intersection of our business proposition and their specific needs.

This is where the timeless "positioning" comes in. A positioning statement keeps an organization on task. And it creates clarity among your employees and your customers as to how you will serve your customers well.

The positioning statement identifies:

- Your target customers
- Your business
- The benefits you offer your customers
- Why your customers will prefer your products and services

TARGET CUSTOMERS

You must know more about what your customer needs than the customer knows. If you *do* know your customer, and if you *do* bring real value to that customer, the two of you will be doing business for life.

Your target customers are those customers you can serve particularly well, based on your company's strengths. These are the customers who care about what your company cares about—and you care about them.

- If you don't care how you look, you are not a candidate for expensive European fashions, and companies that sell those fashions should not be targeting you.
- If you don't like to read, you should not be a target customer for magazine sales promotions, retail booksellers, or publishers.

People who care about what you care about are more likely to recognize the quality of your product or service offering—and be willing to pay for it. You grow your margins over time by finding a group of customers whom you want to serve, and who want to be served by you. If you are loyal in serving their needs, they will be loyal to you. And you will be able to charge a fair price in any economic climate.

YOUR BUSINESS

Defining your business always sounds so simple—but it isn't. Defining it well allows you to differentiate yourself from competition. A clear definition will help you allocate your resources in a unique manner that serves your customers. You will win customers in new and unusual ways.

Consider Harley-Davidson. What business is it in? Maybe "motorcycles." Maybe "big touring motorcycles." But look at all the Harley events the company sponsors. Maybe it is actually in the "entertainment" business. Any of these business definitions could make sense and provide guidance for future growth. But Harley-Davidson was once owned by AMF, a big sporting goods conglomerate. Along with Harley-Davidson motorcycles, AMF made volleyballs, and outboard motors, and bowling lanes! What true consumer need united those products? None! Eventually that showed up in bottom-line performance. On its own, Harley-Davidson has true clarity about the business it is in.

Remember the Beatrice Company of the 1980s? It owned Stifle lamps and a sausage company. Give me a break! In this case, the company simply got broken up.

Knowing what business you are in is a long-term, viable, consumer-driven way to ensure your investors of a superior return on their investment.

THE BENEFITS YOU OFFER CUSTOMERS

Customers don't really care whether you are in a particular business. They shouldn't care. Your focus is on giving them reasons to care about what is in it for them.

The act of buying starts with a customer need. As the customer considers acting on that need, why should your product be the one she or he selects? Answering that question focuses your efforts on where you make contact with your customers. It is the timeless wisdom of Sun Tzu again: Where do you want to fight for their business? Name your battleground. It is your choice, so pick a spot that is inherently advantageous to your company.

If your costs are not the lowest in your industry, don't pick low prices. Sears and Kmart did that and lost because they had high costs.

If your people are not the best and most motivated, don't pick customer service. Howard Johnson did that—if you don't remember the name, the company operated hotels and restaurants. Its customer service was undistinguished.

If you can find nothing that distinguishes you from the competition, pick something, and make your organization better at that "something" than anyone else.

CUSTOMER PREFERENCE FOR YOUR PRODUCTS AND SERVICES

This is gut-check time on positioning. What is your company really about? When it is time to dig deep, where do you dig?

Why do so many people swear by Dell computers? You can't really go anywhere to see them. They use the same processors as anyone else. Their pricing seems fair, but other computers sell for less. There is something in Dell's overall service and reliability position that makes people fans.

Dell's positioning seriously considers customer service—and customers give the company great credit for its service.

Being a valued lifetime supplier goes beyond delivering a product or service. You need to delight the customer. Whatever it is that makes you a preferred supplier must answer the customer's question, "What does it do for me?"

The customer is the force that drives your business. Think about the customer's problems and how to solve those problems—forget yours.

SIMPLE IDEAS, EXECUTED WITH GUSTO, HAVE A TENDENCY TO WORK

Simplicity powers many good ideas. If an idea is simple, both employees and customers can understand it. Every fiber of your organization can be harnessed to a simple idea.

How does simplicity differentiate your company and build a future? By creating a towering strength your competition can't copy. Simple execution followed by simple execution adds strengths that can be difficult for competitors to emulate.

Southwest Airlines provides good service. It has a strong on-time performance record. Its employees have a great sense of service. A lot of people prefer Southwest to its competitors.

In the Northeast, JetBlue airlines has been creating these same feelings.

What do these two airlines do? They live their mission throughout the workforce; everyone gets involved in getting planes out on time and serving customers. In some areas, however, they do less:

- They fly fewer varieties of planes.
- They serve fewer meals.
- They have less complicated fare structures and fewer fare restrictions.

In these instances, less is more. These airlines screw up fewer things. Have you ever heard anyone complain about the food on Southwest? Nope, since Southwest doesn't serve you a meal. Have you ever heard anyone complain about a seat assignment on Southwest? Nope; Southwest doesn't have assigned seating. Do you hear people complain about being late on Southwest? Not nearly as much as people do on other airlines; operating just one kind of aircraft has contributed to historically strong on-time performance—and lower operating costs.

Southwest and JetBlue don't have the best frequent flyer program. They don't have the most destinations. But they sure are building customer loyalty.

Wal-Mart is now the largest company in the world. In survey after survey, customers say they don't like its service, and they don't like the conditions of its stores. Wal-Mart customers don't like the congestion of its parking lots. Customers like just one thing: the prices.

Wal-Mart's success is built on the customers' perception that it delivers good prices on everything from lawn mowers to dish detergent to blue jeans. Through a combination of logistical efficiency and technological prowess, Wal-Mart is able to move shelf-stable goods to customers at a low cost. In those areas, Wal-Mart thrives and grows.

Wegmans Food Markets is popular in the Northeast among customers who like to cook or have a high appreciation for food. Over time, the company built this image—one program at a time. The prepared foods areas are an example. First, Wegmans offered Chinese food, prepared authentically in-store. Next, it offered hot meals to go at a few stores. And over time, with some experimentation, that worked. Later came in-store quality pizza shops. And after that, sub shops. Still later, French patisseries were added for dessert. This is simple execution, followed by simple execution, all targeted (and relevant) to the same customers.

ARE CUSTOMERS MAKING SACRIFICES TO PURCHASE YOUR BRAND?

The best indicator of loyalty is whether your customers are making a specific effort to purchase your brand. How do you identify whether customers are making sacrifices for your brand? Not big sacrifices, but little, everyday inconveniences.

If you are a retailer, are customers driving a little farther to shop at your stores—maybe occasionally driving past a competitor to get to you? Then you are building customer loyalty.

If you are a manufacturer of consumer goods, are your end customers reaching past your competitors' products to get your goods? Will your customers change where they shop in order to get your brand? If so, you are building customer loyalty.

If you are a business-to-business marketer, are your customers willing to pay more for your product than for a competitor's? If so, you are building customer loyalty.

Sandy Beal, the chief executive officer of Ruby Tuesday's restaurants, says his customer service creed is, "The answer is yes. Now, what's the question?"

FIND OUT WHAT THE CUSTOMER THINKS

Don't prioritize according to your needs. Don't guess about the customer's priorities. Ask your customer about his or her priorities, then prioritize your actions according to your customers' needs. Talking to your customers on a regular basis is common sense, and doesn't cost much.

At Hyatt hotels, the executives become bellhops and waiters for 1 week each year in order to reach out and touch the customer. At Procter & Gamble's product manager seminars, one day is spent talking to customers in stores. Why is it that actions like these are not common and that people are always so surprised at what they learn when they talk to customers?

Because marketing people know customers, marketing people know the direction the compass is pointing for future business.

Don't get into the rut of fixing the same customer problems over and over again. Get the information from customers concerning shortcomings into a form that your organization can use to improve its performance. Continuous improvement, driven by feedback from customers, is a fundamental component of good marketing.

If what you are doing is not providing benefits that customers recognize, stop doing it. Forget the dollars you have spent to provide the product or service. It's not the way you've always done it that counts. What counts is what the customer wants.

Explore with your customers where you are falling short (they will probably give you credit just for listening!). Turn the problem into a positive by showing customers how responsive your company can be.

Without the loyalty of your customers, your business doesn't have a secure source of future profits. It all starts with your customers.

It's simple but true: Happy customers come back again and again and again.

Second Principle
Organization of Intelligence

What is needed in war
is to obtain the name of the enemy leader
and decide on his capacity,
so as to calculate what his plans will be
and make use of this survey
to obtain success without great difficulty.

—"Wu Chi on *The Art of War*"
Third Century B.C.

> **STRATEGICALLY**
> Intelligence reduces surprise and focuses plans.
>
> **TACTICALLY**
> Intelligence helps you take calculated risks.

Know your market as well as you know yourself.

 Military commanders are divided over whether good intelligence or a sound objective is the primary consideration for success. In marketing, there is no question about it. This often-repeated story about the dog food that isn't selling tells it all: At a meeting where members of the headquarters staff are trying to determine why the dog food isn't selling, various reasons for the lack of business are presented. One bureaucrat says it's poor packaging; another blames bad advertising. All kinds of imagined weaknesses are suggested. Finally, someone who has been out in the market points out that the real reason why the dog food isn't selling is that *the dogs don't like it*. The lesson: The market is the best source of information. Marketing research is the business system that helps you determine the market for your products and services.

The German field manual *Command of Troops says*, "Confusion concerning the situation is a normal state of affairs. Only rarely will exact details of the enemy be known. While the attempt to find out about him is a matter of course, waiting for news in a bad situation is a bad error."

A good formal and informal intelligence system coupled with good marketing practices puts you in the business of managing risks instead of taking risks.

INFORMATION PROCESSING SYSTEMS

Organizing, synthesizing, and disseminating information is a major problem in every organization. Most companies are plagued with "islands of information." Many people know many things, but no system exists to put it all together for verification and application to specific objectives.

Uncertainty surrounds many of the issues that challenge the customer-driven leader. The antidote for uncertainty is more relevant information. However, more information requires more processing time, and not all information is useful. Too much information can make it difficult to separate the useful from the useless.

The ultimate solution is a combination of

- Structures that size the decision making
- Good information at all levels
- Personal reconnaissance on the part of the ultimate decision maker
- A predisposition to take action on information gained

With good intelligence systems, we make the invisible become visible. Successful strategy needs good information. Good information is a product of good intelligence. Whatever warnings we're going to get about the future, we already have. Analysis of major events proves that maxim. Postmortems of the World Trade Center disaster or the breakup of the shuttle *Columbia* indicate that critical information was ignored. The problem is sifting through the data prior to any incident to determine which information is critical for taking the correct preventive course of action.

If you try to make a computer smarter by giving it more information, it takes longer to process the information and provide the answer. While the brain has more components than a computer, the brain is slower. And like the computer, the brain can suffer from information overload.

With computers, the solution to the need for more capability is to break the problem into segments and look at each segment separately. With people, the solution is a similar decentralization: You break the problem down and have decisions made by people at each level instead of sending all the information to the top, where it will overload the head person's brain.

Organizing your intelligence input helps you achieve flexibility in adjusting your plan to the real world. How does the information relate to the critical objectives you are trying to accomplish? How will you monitor unexpected events and your opponent's actions?

Failure to organize the input leaves you and your organization in the position of sifting through data that are not relevant. Time and opportunities are lost.

Accurate information is the bedrock of the road to business success. First, you decide who you want your customers to be. Then, you decide what these customers need and want. You figure out which of these needs you can meet, and you do it better than anyone else. Note the need for information in this simplified illustration of the road to success.

Intelligence is not about spying. Only a small percentage of the CIA budget goes to covert operations. Much of what you want to know is readily available or can be uncovered by listening to your customers.

Make a Thorough Assessment

*To make an assessment
of the outcome of a war,
one must compare the various conditions
of the antagonistic sides.*
—Sun Tzu

ASSESS YOUR MARKETING OPPORTUNITY

Sun Tzu lists five assessment factors that have modern marketing management equivalents:

1. *Moral influence.* Great strategies flow from visions and missions that have a strong moral foundation. Victory is often on the side of what is right.
2. *Weather.* Every marketing plan must consider the influence of outside forces, such as economic conditions, government regulations, political circumstances, and the environment.
3. *Terrain.* Where and how you address the market is covered by the "eight Ps": planning, people, products, positioning, promotion, persuasion, personal selling, and price.
4. *Commander.* Sun Tzu states the importance of wisdom, sincerity, benevolence, courage, and strictness (discipline). The same personal qualities are important today. The strong leader who communicates a strong vision prevails.
5. *Doctrine.* The core beliefs and values of the leaders form the culture of the organization. A strategy usually cannot kill a culture, but a culture can kill a strategy.

ANALYZE STRENGTHS, WEAKNESSES, OPPORTUNITIES, AND THREATS

The need for thorough study and assessment before the battle is often ignored in the rush to action. An internal and external analysis generates the foundation for a clear written statement of the vision and mission of the organization.

If you bring in someone from the outside to solve a problem or help your organization grow, the first thing that person will need to do is conduct an assessment. That is, she or he will need to find out what is happening and what is not happening internally, and to find out what critical external factors in the market affect your product or service.

Here are a few common interview questions used in an internal assessment:

- What are the most pressing concerns (major challenges) facing this organization?
- If you could change anything, what would you change about the company and/or your function?
- What must people be sure to do and not do?
- How much latitude do people have to try new ideas, and can they make mistakes?
- What are you most proud of in your company, in your area, and personally?
- How are major functional relationships working?
- If you and others were working better as a team, what different things would be happening?
- If you were to describe your company as an animal—beast, fish, or fowl—what animal would it be?

Almost 100 years ago, a discerning general wrote, "Why do these officers always want to move their headquarters to the rear? They say it is so they can get a view of what is happening. All they can see is what is around them!"

The tendency to see only what is around us, or what is provided to us to see, is still true. Organizational assessments and questionnaires can uncover new information and reveal new threats and opportunities.

Any marketing plan should be preceded by a SWOT analysis. The acronym stands for strengths, weaknesses, opportunities, and threats.

Internal analysis:

- *Strengths:* Internal core competencies that lead to competitive advantages
- *Weaknesses:* Internal characteristics that limit the effectiveness of your organization

External analysis:

- *Opportunities:* External issues indicating new directions in which to utilize resources to enhance performance
- *Threats:* External areas of concern that may directly or indirectly affect your business

This analysis provides the basis for discussions to determine the major strategic thrusts of your organization.

Knowledge Is Marketing Power

Thus the saying:
Know the enemy and know yourself,
and your victory will never be endangered;
know the weather and know the ground,
and your victory will then be complete.

Now, the commander who gets many scores during the calculations in the temple before the war will have more likelihood of winning. The commander who gets few scores during the calculations in the temple before the war will have less chance of success. With many scores, one can win; with few scores, one cannot. How much less chance of victory has someone who gets no scores at all! By examining the situation through these aspects, I can foresee who is likely to win or lose.

—Sun Tzu

"When I took a decision, or adopted an alternative, it was after studying every relevant—and many an irrelevant—factor. Geography, tribal structure, religion, social customs, language, appetites, standards—all were at my finger-ends. The enemy I knew almost like my own side. I risked myself among them a hundred times to learn."

—T. E. Lawrence, 1933

A colonel of the German General Staff writes: "A man who is not continually and unintermittently working at himself and the training of his mind, has not heard a whisper of the dynamics of our life."

SECOND PRINCIPLE

LEARN FROM
THE EXPERIENCE
OF OTHERS

"That men do not learn very much from the lessons of history is the most important of all the lessons that history has to offer."
—Aldous Huxley

All great captains have won because they looked both ahead *and* back. They looked back and reviewed the actions of their predecessors in similar circumstances. As they looked ahead, these captains used this information to develop strategies and tactics that achieved their objectives. They did not copy, they learned. Copying misses the subtleties that are so important to success. Many businesses are "me too." Copying from your competitor can take you in the wrong direction.

Speaking of officers who rely only on practical experience, Frederick the Great said, "The Prussian commissariat department has two mules which have served through 20 campaigns—but they are mules still."

Bismarck said, "Fools say they learn by experience. I prefer to learn by other people's experience." For the marketer, military lessons provide a fresh approach. The business mind can roam through concepts and develop winning strategies. Because the military and business share a common strategic language, military lessons can readily be transformed into business lessons. The process of taking experiences from an alien discipline and applying them to our own provides fresh insights that lead to new solutions.

The lessons for marketers are found in case studies, conferences, and books. Establish a strategy for growth in marketing knowledge for yourself and your staff. When you find a good book, give a copy to each member of your staff. I've found that a good way to get people immersed in the book is to pass it out at a conference and have each person read a page out loud in round-robin fashion until we've covered the first 20 pages. This gets people into the meat of the book and increases the possibility they will read more.

Good Research
Is Critical

The reason
the enlightened sovereign and wise general
conquer the enemy whenever they move
and their achievements
surpass those of ordinary men
is they have foreknowledge.

This "foreknowledge" cannot be elicited from spirits, nor from gods, nor by analogy with past events, nor by any deductive calculations. It must be obtained from the men who know the enemy situation.

Hence, the use of spies, of whom there are five sorts: native spies, internal spies, converted spies, doomed spies, and surviving spies. When all these five sorts of spies are at work and none knows their method of operation, it would be divinely intricate and constitutes the greatest treasure of a sovereign.

1. *Native spies are those we employ from the enemy's country people.*
2. *Internal spies are enemy officials whom we employ.*
3. *Converted spies are enemy spies whom we employ.*
4. *Doomed spies are those of our own spies who are deliberately given false information and told to report it.*
5. *Surviving spies are those who return from the enemy camp to report information.*

- *Of all those in the army close to the commander, none is more intimate than the spies.*
- *Of all rewards, none is more liberal than those given to spies.*

- *Of all matters, none is more confidential than those relating to spying operations.*

He who is not sage cannot use spies. He who is not humane and generous cannot use spies. And he who is not delicate and subtle cannot get the truth out of them. Delicate indeed! Truly delicate!
—Sun Tzu

Some predictions are right.
- Jules Verne's vision of a trip to the moon was close to the actual Apollo 11 makeup. Verne described the proper crew size of three and the launch site of Florida, and came within 17 inches of estimating the correct length of the spacecraft.

Some are wrong.
- IBM chairman Thomas J. Watson made a prediction in 1943 that there was a world market for "about five computers."
- Noted surgeon Alfred Velpeau dismissed anesthesia in 1839 when he said, "Knife and pain are two words in surgery that must forever be associated."

Von Clausewitz said, "A great part of the information obtained in war is contradictory, a still greater part is false, and by far the greatest part is of doubtful character."

A GOOD RESEARCH PROGRAM KEEPS YOU INFORMED

America's successful organizations treat research as a corporate asset because it helps them market more efficiently and effectively. FedEx is a product of market research—founder Fred Smith wrote a college paper on his idea and turned it into a successful company. His Yale professor wrote, "The concept is interesting and well formed, but in order to earn better than a C, the idea must be feasible."

A good research analyst can have the misfortune of spotting bad news before others do—and must defend his or her conclusions. Research requires the expertise of three professions:

1. *Detective:* Accurately determining what the client wants and finding the raw data.
2. *Analyst:* Doing the analysis. This includes perceiving the decision maker's bias.
3. *Politician:* Following up the analysis with an effective rebuttal of the decision maker's invalid objections.

Indeed, confronting senior managers when the information is negative can be tough work. How difficult it is to find critical truths and get them received by decision makers. The enemy comprises those who tell management what it wants to hear. How sad it is to hear someone reject input by offering comments that deny the value of the information. Input from marketing research focuses discussions on what customers want—not what management thinks customers want. The "facts" that originate from the research customer's mind are subject to interpretation (and misinterpretation) based on the receiver's personal bias.

Management discussions based on customer-focused research can make it easier to accomplish organizational change.

At the Coach organization, production of new leather products and accessories is determined with the aid of customer research. The company has spent about $2 million annually on customer research. In addition to questions about style and comfort, customers are asked to rank new designs against existing items. Finally, products are tested in stores before a national launch.

Benchmarking is a useful research methodology that focuses on learning from any organization with the same processes. The goal is process superiority.

Know Your Market

*It is the highest responsibility of the general
to inquire into the nature of the ground with utmost care.*

*It is necessary for the wise general to make correct assessments of the
enemy's situation to create conditions leading to victory and to calculate distances and the degree of difficulty of the terrain.*

*He who knows these things and applies them to fighting will defi-
nitely win. He who knows them not, and, therefore, is unable to apply
them, will definitely lose.*

*One ignorant of the designs of neighboring states cannot enter into
alliances with them; if ignorant of the conditions of mountains, forests,
dangerous defiles, swamps, and marshes, he cannot conduct the march
of an army; if he fails to make use of native guides, he cannot gain the
advantages of ground.*

—Sun Tzu

Frederick the Great wrote in *Instructions for His Generals,* "If it is
not in time of war, the places are visited, camps are chosen, roads
are examined, the mayors of the villages, the butchers, and the
farmers are talked to. One becomes familiar with the footpaths,
the depths of the woods, their nature, the depth of the rivers, the
marshes that can be crossed and those which cannot . . .

KNOW WHAT YOUR MARKET WANTS TODAY AND TOMORROW

I've found the best information about "the market" when I've
penetrated the layers of management in my customer's organi-

28

zation and reached people on the front line. This penetration took me beyond my customer to my customer's customer—and to useful ideas for a new offensive.

The best way to attain the offensive is to spend "face time" with your best customers and prospects at their places of business. That puts you in the position of being master of the situation.

Look at any successful retailing organization. Where do the company leaders spend a good portion of their time? They spend it in their stores, listening to what their employees and customers are saying. These leaders want to see how their programs and procedures are implemented at the store level, so that fine-tuning adjustments can be made as required.

Customers are willing to spend money (and time) on those products and categories that are truly important to them. In the nineteeth century the average American spent 50 percent of his or her income on food. Today, she or he spends less than 10 percent on food. Where are consumers spending that other 40 percent? Where they want to spend it. The average millionaire spends just $3800 more for a new car than the average American spends. That's not a big difference when one considers the differences in purchasing power.

Customers will spend their money in areas that are important to them. For example, a Boston cabbie I met purchased only organic food and ate only at organic restaurants! He is a prime target customer in the organic food industry.

Knowing your customer is not just about knowing your demographics and what your "average" looks like. Tom Peters, coauthor of *In Search of Excellence*, calls personal observation "management by walking around." In the marketing profession, it is more like "marketing by wallowing around." This is a process that can draw people together regardless of position as they look at data and insert observations. These "gut checks" should be scheduled regularly, with the objective of seeing the real world as it is and will be.

The observation and analysis answers these simple questions:

1. What is happening?
2. What is not happening?
3. What do I wish was happening?
4. What can I do to make a difference?

The objective is not to make a decision on the spot, but rather to get a feel for the market so that data can be understood when analyzing field reports. Nothing substitutes for "knowing your customers," having a gut feel for what they really want and why they want it.

The first paragraph of any plan should always be devoted to the needs of the customer.

Prepare a Competitive Analysis

*To forecast the outcome of a war
the attributes of the antagonistic sides should be analyzed.*

Make the following comparisons:

1. *Which sovereign possesses greater moral influence?*
2. *Which commander is more capable?*
3. *Which side holds more favorable conditions in weather and terrain?*
4. *On which side are decrees better implemented?*
5. *Which side is superior in arms?*
6. *On which side are officers and men better trained?*
7. *Which side is stricter and more impartial in meting out rewards and punishments?*

By means of these seven elements, I can forecast victory or defeat.
If the sovereign heeds these stratagems of mine and acts upon them, he will surely win the war, and I shall, therefore, stay with him. If the sovereign neither heeds nor acts upon them, he will certainly suffer defeat, and I shall leave.

—Sun Tzu

TAKE A LOOK.
TAKE A
GOOD LOOK!

When Marriott designed Fairfield Inns, it wanted a product that would beat the competition. Teams were sent to check out competitors' hotel rooms. The information gleaned from headhunters hiring new personnel revealed competitors' pay, training, and benefit packages.

KNOW YOUR COMPETITORS
AS ORGANIZATIONS AND AS PEOPLE

Here are ways you can "mine" for information.

Competitive Profile

The best competitive analysis profiles not only the company but also the characteristics of the top decision makers. When you truly understand your competitor as a person, you can more easily predict her or his future courses of action. Your battle is between two human intelligences, not two corporate cadres.

Look at both the competitive issues and the personalities. What happened in prior circumstances? Look at the personalities in terms of their background and experience—where did they get their business lessons; what have they done in similar situations?

In the armies of the world, the personality profile intelligence is called the "order of battle." It explores the personal characteristics of the opposing commanders. You have seen the effects of personalities in the heavy footprints of new senior managers.

Competitive Comparisons

This analysis reveals competitive strengths, weaknesses, and costs. Your customers are comparing your products and services to those of your competitor. You must also make similar comparisons in order to achieve competitive superiority.

Mentally place yourself in a competitor's company and prepare a brief written analysis of "your company." From this document, design a template for analyzing your major competitors.

It is through the analysis of competitive information that you determine how and where you can penetrate the market. This information tells you as much about what you cannot do as what you can do.

As you compare yourself to your competitors, the emerging analysis should reveal comparative advantages that are key criteria for designing a strategy focused on your strengths.

Some managers keep a log of all intelligence and pricing reports from the field. This helps them develop a perspective on trends. These data can help convince senior management of the need for change or contradict the isolated erroneous reports that reach the top. It's all part of both knowing what you are doing *and* looking as if you know what you are doing.

Study the Signals

When the trees are seen to move,
it means the enemy is advancing.

- *When many screens have been placed in the undergrowth, it is for the purpose of deception.*
- *When the enemy's envoys speak in humble terms, but the army continues preparations, that means it will advance.*
- *When their language is strong and the enemy pretentiously drives forward, these may be signs that he will retreat.*
- *When the enemy is not in dire straits but asks for a truce, he must be plotting.*
- *When light chariots first go out and take positions on the wings, it is a sign that the enemy is forming for battle.*
- *When his troops march speedily and parade in formations, he is expecting to fight a decisive battle on a fixed date.*
- *When the enemy sees an advantage but does not advance to seize it, he is fatigued.*

—Sun Tzu

The master encourages personal observation and analysis.

MATCH YOUR PERSONAL OBSERVATION WITH FORMAL RESEARCH

The failures of intelligence systems are not failures of "the system" but rather failures of managers who misunderstand and misuse the system.

It's too easy to engage in internal conjecture. John Z. DeLorean, a former General Motors executive famed for his iconoclastic remarks, once said, "All group vice presidents do is sit around and talk to each other."

Nothing substitutes for a combination of hard data and personal observation. Perception and judgment go hand in hand. If you want to make good judgments, you must have accurate perceptions of the market. If you have accurate perceptions, you can make good judgments.

A single observation is simply one data point—and you require more than that to make an informed decision. In the absence of good data, executives waste time arguing their opinions. People, not issues, become the focus of disagreement, and interpersonal conflict results. Facts quickly guide people to the central issues.

The primary information focus should be on what the customer wants and needs. A companion focus should be on the product, in order to create what the customer wants and needs. The result is a winning marriage of information and action. The trap is thinking about marketing in terms of only the product or only the customer—winners consider balancing a product focus with a customer focus.

Protect Your Secrets

*There is no place
where espionage is not possible.*

It is essential to seek out enemy spies who have come to conduct espionage against you and bribe them to serve you. Courteously exhort them and give your instructions, then release them back home.
—Sun Tzu

TOYS TODAY; TOMORROW YOUR PRODUCTS?

Today, China makes 70 percent of the world's toys and accounts for almost 50 percent of the counterfeits seized in the United States by the Customs Service. The problem has worsened with the development of so-called rapid prototypes, which can take a three-dimensional computer scan of a toy and reproduce it within hours.

The world's largest toymakers don't even have an exhibit at the Hong Kong toy fair, but small toymakers do not have that option. Mattel holds its own invitation-only toy fairs for distributors and retailers.

THERE IS NO PLACE WHERE ESPIONAGE IS NOT POSSIBLE

The business world is filled with people who can relate how they got useful information simply by calling and asking questions.

Countless people who call on you also go into the enemy camp. Do not trust the supplier, editor, or any other itinerant traveler who relates information about your competitors. The visitor who divulges competitive information is providing the same intelligence service to your competition.

In the new world of concern about terrorists, business security has moved to a much higher level. However, while it has become more difficult for strangers to wander through your offices, be careful of "friends" who do business with you.

If you do not give false information to your vendors, you can at least take careful, deliberate steps to keep them from learning what is going on in your business.

Some information within your company should be compartmentalized on a need-to-know basis. It's not that you don't trust your own people, but that your staff will be offered opportunities for job interviews with your competitors. I recall working for a corporate president who kept abreast of industry activities by regularly granting job interviews to senior executives of competing companies.

Espionage happens at every level. A restaurant owner tells about the missing recipe book and the inquisitive employee who gave his secret ingredients to a competitor down the street.

When one family member works for one company and another family member is employed at a competitor, this can be a source of leaks of tactical information, such as weekly sales plans and company newspapers.

By far the largest theft of corporate secrets is through the computer and the Internet. We regularly read about government secrets being stolen and offered for sale. Why should we think things are any different in our business?

Third Principle
Maintenance of the Objective

*What is called method is returning to the beginning
to obtain the fundamental things.*

*What is called right is acquiring efficiency
by the practice of things.*

*What is called planning
is avoiding damage and gaining advantage.*

—"Wu Chi on *The Art of War*"
Third Century B.C.

STRATEGICALLY
The objective provides one main direction.

TACTICALLY
The objective is a specific goal.

A clear intention and a steady aim.

 Some strategists believe that the objective is the most important principle because without an objective, all of the other principles are pointless. The objective is intertwined with the strategy.

In the *Chief Executive's Handbook,* Kenneth Andrews says that strategy combines what a company

Might do in terms of alternatives
Can do in terms of resources and power
Wants to do in terms of management values and goals
Ought to do in terms of responsibility to society

Those four points make a good window for determining your objectives and strategy.

The objective determines the "what," and the other principles guide the "how."

Get your objective right from the start. The business objective must be clearly defined, decisive, and attainable. Actions must be clearly communicated, and results must be measurable.

THE OBJECTIVE IS CLEARLY DEFINED

The People's Republic of China places great emphasis on singleness of direction. Its rule is that, strategically, there must be only one main direction, and, tactically, there must be a single objective.

Unquestionably, there must be singleness of purpose and simplicity in the objective. In one American company, the rule is that having more than one objective is having no objective.

The objective should be so simply stated that it can pass the "3-by-5 test." That is, you should be able to write it on a 3-by-5 index card.

The objective should be stated in specific terms that are measurable. You should always know whether or not you have achieved the objective by listing goals that can be identified. *Improve* is too general a term without a specific measurable number. *As soon as possible* is too vague.

THE OBJECTIVE IS DECISIVE

"Only great battles produce great results. . . . Pursue one great decisive aim with force and determination," says Clausewitz.

The statement of the objective must be targeted toward a goal that is strategically and tactically meaningful. Attainment of your objective should contribute significantly to the fulfillment of your long-range plans—your corporate mission. There are a lot of interesting things you can do; focus on objectives that make a difference. Your purpose is not to merely engage the competition; you want to win!

In industries where the pace of business moves rapidly, it is possible to set objectives that represent a substantial increase in business and result in a loss of market share in the industry. The solution is to focus on achieving decisive objectives in new, emerging segments of the industry.

THE OBJECTIVE IS ATTAINABLE

The objective must be a "stretch" that is consistent with the capability of the organization. Objectives that are impossible can demoralize. Conversely, objectives that are too easy to attain are useless.

The statement of the objective should allow the organization to choose side roads, as long as they do not lead to a dead end.

The process of communicating the objective should set up the interactive communications necessary for attainment. If your culture allows subordinates to tell you what they cannot do, then you have the opportunity to engage in a dialogue to determine feasibility and make adjustments in motivation, guidance, or resources.

The reason you have an objective is to clarify where you are going so you can get everyone marching in the same direction. If your command does not provide the moral and physical means to attain the objective, then your objective will not be attained.

"Maintenance of the objective" means choosing a strategic direction or tactical goal and sticking with it. We often operate with limited information. As the situation develops, there is a temptation to change objectives. This is confusing and wastes time and energy. History teaches that the organization most likely to succeed is the one that consistently pursues its original aim.

In Vietnam, it was possible to identify 22 different American rationales, compared to a single North Vietnamese objective—the conquest of South Vietnam. Our plan was for the next battle; theirs was for years ahead.

THE OBJECTIVE IS
CLEARLY COMMUNICATED

Over and over again, military commanders make the point that the objective must be carefully formulated by the commander and clearly communicated to subordinate commanders, and by them to their subordinates. Everyone must know where he or she is going, when he or she is expected to arrive, and what he or she must achieve.

Clausewitz says, "Once it has been decided . . . what the war is about, and what it can do, the way to do it is easily found. But to follow the way unerringly, to carry a plan through, not to be distracted a thousand times by a thousand inducements—that calls for strength of character, assurance, and clearness of mind."

Long ago, Neutrogena sighted a viable objective and refused to blink. Every step that Neutrogena took was designed to position the brand as a cohesive line of luxury skin-care products worth a premium price. The soap was given to doctors so they could give samples to consumers. Neutrogena gave doctors a mild, reliable soap; doctors gave Neutrogena credibility. To enhance the luxury aura, an aggressive hotel sampling program was carried out in deluxe hotels. Today the Neutrogena brand name has high name recognition, matched with high customer loyalty.

Find
a Winning
Strategy

---

*A triumphant army
will not fight until victory is assured.*

*An army destined to defeat
will always fight with the opponent first,
in the hope that it may win by sheer good luck.*

To foresee a victory no better than ordinary people's foresight is not the acme of excellence. Neither is it the acme of excellence if you win a victory through fierce fighting and the whole empire says, "Well done!" Hence, by analogy, to lift an autumn hair [hare] does not signify great strength; to see the sun and moon does not signify good sight; to hear the thunderclap does not signify acute hearing.

In ancient times, those called skilled in war conquered an enemy easily conquered. Consequently, a master of war wins victories without showing his brilliant military success, and without gaining the reputation for wisdom or the merit for valor. He wins his victories without making mistakes. Making no mistakes is what establishes the certainty of victory, for it means that he conquers an enemy already defeated.

—Sun Tzu

"Strategy wins victories, but only when crowned by tactical success at the end of each move or series of moves."

—John G. Burr
The Framework of Battle

STRATEGY BEFORE TACTICS

Of all the maxims in *The Art of War*, "fighting when victory is assured" is among the most significant and useful because it clearly states that the way to win must be determined before the battle. Without a strategy that is well thought out in advance, we will struggle for a way to win.

This concept of strategy before tactics applies to every situation—thinking comes before doing.

Here is how strategy differs from tactics:

Strategy is a planning process.   Tactics is a contact process.
Strategy is "war on paper."   Tactics is the actual battle.
Strategy is doing the right thing. Tactics is doing things right.
Strategy is a mental process.   Tactics involves action.

- Whenever you are planning, you are engaged in strategy. The key word that differentiates tactics from strategy is "contact." Whenever anyone at any level is in "contact" with the customer, that person is engaged in tactics.
- Strategy deals with the allocation of resources to the marketing battle. Strategic principles are constant and do not change with the times.
- Tactics deals with the use of resources in battle. Tactics is the execution of strategy in the real world—and must constantly be tuned to current conditions. Napoleon said that an army is not of good quality unless it changes tactics every 10 years.

The marketing process determines the consumer-driven strategy; the selling process engages in tactics to deliver the product or service to the end customer. If you have not done your strategy (marketing) well, then your only hope is to be saved by superior tactics (selling or merchandising).

The best organizations develop both winning marketing and selling. That is, they do their marketing so well that they are sure to win, and when competitive forces are encountered, their selling is so good that they win anyway. There is no better example of a winning strategy than Wal-Mart's strategy of situating discount stores in small towns and wholesale clubs in large cities— an excellent example of complementary strategies that do not compete with each other. Both sell highly identifiable brand names at a discount.

History does not tolerate errors in the design of the strategic master plan. Victory is determined by the strategy established *before* entering the market.

The critical duty of marketing is to provide the concepts and merchandising for products that meet the customers' needs.

The Supreme Excellence is to Win without Fighting

Generally, in war the best thing of all
is to take the enemy's state whole and intact;
to ruin it is an inferior strategy.

To capture the enemy's entire army is better than to destroy it; to take intact a battalion, a company or a five-man squad is better than to destroy them. Hence, to win 100 victories in 100 battles is not the acme of skill. To subdue the enemy without fighting is the supreme excellence.

- *Thus, the best policy in war is to attack the enemy's strategy.*
- *The second best way is to disrupt its alliances through diplomatic means.*
- *The next best method is to attack its army in the field.*

The worst policy is to attack walled cities. Attacking cities is the last resort, used only when there is no alternative.

It takes at least three months to make mantlets and shielded vehicles ready and prepare necessary arms and equipment. It takes at least another three months to pile up earthen mounds against the walls. The general unable to control his impatience will order his troops to swarm up the wall like ants with the result that one-third of them are slain, while the cities remain untaken. Such is the calamity of attacking walled cities.

Therefore, those skilled in war subdue the enemy's army without fighting. They capture the enemy's cities without assaulting them and overthrow his state without protracted operations.

Their aim must be to take all under heaven intact through strategic superiority. Thus, their troops are not worn out and their triumph will be complete. This is the art of attacking by stratagem.

—Sun Tzu

"The highest type of strategy—sometimes called grand strategy—is that which so integrates the policies and armaments of the nation that the resort to war is either rendered unnecessary or is undertaken with the maximum chance of victory."

—Edward Meade Earle
Makers of Modern Strategy, 1944

THE SIDE THAT WINS WILL PROBABLY BE THE SIDE THAT HAS ALREADY WON

That is, the winning side will have done their strategy so well that opposition is discouraged from fighting.

A business strategy that wins without fighting either

- Terrorizes potential new competitors so they never enter the market.

or

- Defeats existing competition. At one extreme, the market entry is not realized as a threat until too late; at the other extreme, the execution of the entry strategy overwhelms competitors.

The supreme excellence in marketing strategy is to attack the competitor's plans. The supreme excellence in negotiating strategy is to find a way for both sides to win.

In Switzerland, in World War I, General Ulrich Willie led the Swiss to victory—that is, a victory that consisted of successfully avoiding conflict. Again, in World War II, General Henri Guisan led the Swiss to victory; as someone put it, "We won by having no war."

One could say that Switzerland does not have an army with trained, able-bodied civilians who keep weapons and ammo in their homes, Switzerland is an army. The best marketing companies do not just have a marketing department; they are marketing armies with a marketing attitude that often wins customers without fighting. You know about these companies, because they are the ones you contact to make a purchase.

The big box retailers often win without fighting. Like the Mongol invaders that swept through Europe, the giant bookstores, home improvement stores, office supply stores and other supersize specialty retailers have a reputation for gobbling up so much business that smaller retailers immediately vacate the market. I can recall conversations with an independent hardware store owner and a bookseller who knew the giants were coming. In both cases, they predicted their own demise. Survivors in these "customer raids" have found a convenience or service niche that appeals to a select group of customers.

The ultimate marketing strategy is attained with a product or service that is so unique it has no competition. In these circumstances, consider the following alternatives.

- Price your product or service very high in order to maximize profits before others enter the market. The problem is that the perceived high profit potential attracts a lot of competition.

or

- Price your product very low in order to discourage competition. That is, take a low profit margin (and a high market share) that you hope to maintain over a longer period.

Smaller companies will most often go for profit. Larger companies, knowing they have the resources to be a factor, will usually price to keep competition out of the market. Keep in mind that in today's world markets, new low cost competition can arise from unexpected sources.

Look for Strategic Turns

The commander
must create a helpful situation
over and beyond the ordinary rules.

By "situation" I mean
he should act expediently in accordance
with what is advantageous in the field
and so meet any exigency.
—Sun Tzu

STRATEGIC TURNS CHANGE THE COURSE OF HISTORY

In 1066, William, Duke of Normandy invaded England, going up against a formidable opponent. One of the reasons he had confidence in such a risky undertaking was that he had a new way of fighting battles.

Following tradition, the English forces that had horses rode to the battlefield but fought on foot, while the Norman cavalry walked to the location and then mounted for battle. Historians differ as to whether it was the relatively new technology of the stirrup or the existence of a mounted cavalry that afforded the Normans the victory. They do agree that this Battle of Hastings was a turning point both in how battles would be fought and in the course of history.

Later, the rifle initiated another strategic turn in the way battles were fought. However, the horse was too unstable a platform for the rifle, which became the weapon of the foot soldier.

Another strategic turn occurred when the concept of disciplined troops marching in solid lines became outmoded by new weapons and battle tactics.

MARKETS EVOLVE; NEW PRODUCTS EMERGE; THE WORLD MOVES ON

Be aware of strategic turns—also known as paradigm shifts—that can affect your business. Today we are seeing a strategic turn in military strategy with the growing importance of special forces and precision bombing. We are seeing it in communications with the rise of the Internet.

The auto drove buggy-whip manufacturers out of business. Mass merchants like Wal-Mart, Barnes & Noble, and Lowe's take business from small independents. The corner grocer was replaced by the superstore, which is now threatened by mass merchants. The hardware store has been smothered by the home improvement giant.

The strategic turn can arise from outside of your business world. Technology has created entirely new business opportunities. The typewriter has been replaced by the computer, the new daily organizer is the Personal Data Assistant, and the electronic calculator evolved from outside the industry.

You can sell into any market in the world, and competitors from any market in the world can sell into your market. The problem is that the market opportunity keeps changing, and too often we miss the strategic turn. I recall facilitating a strategic planning session in a company where all had done their homework well. A competitive analysis revealed that one of the major competitors had initiated a new international distribution system. Although the emerging pattern of a new distribution system was visible to me as an outsider, the management group was too focused on what had been and couldn't see the strategic turn taking place. After I called time and refocused the discussion, they saw the emerging threat.

At one time, all computers were sold through retail stores and sales forces, then Michael Dell initiated a strategic turn in direct distribution. Hundreds of computer stores closed.

An organization called Fotomat had thousands of yellow and blue kiosks in parking lots offering 24-hour film processing. Then 1-hour processing became the fastest-growing segment of the market, and supermarkets and drugstores installed their own processing centers. Along came the digital camera, and the rest is history.

THIRD PRINCIPLE

Establish Strategic Initiatives

*Pursue one's own strategic designs
to overawe the enemy.*

*Then one can take the enemy's cities and
overthrow the enemy's state.*

When an invincible army attacks a powerful state, it makes it impossible for the enemy to assemble his forces. It overawes the enemy and prevents his allies from joining him. It follows that one does not need to seek alliances with other neighboring states, nor is there any need to foster the power of other states.

—Sun Tzu

MAKING STRATEGIC INITIATIVES WORK

Criteria for assessing a strategic initiative are

- Is it consistent with the strategic direction?
- Is it challenging but achievable?
- Do resources balance with objectives?
- Will the results make a difference?
- Is the responsibility for implementing the initiative assigned to a manager with sufficient authority?

SELECT STRATEGIC INITIATIVES THAT WILL MAKE A DIFFERENCE

The strategic initiative is where you will concentrate efforts. Often, less is more. That is, a few initiatives will concentrate efforts, whereas too many initiatives will scatter efforts.

Here are a few basic principles of marketing you should consider when establishing strategic initiatives. Note that none of these are mutually exclusive. For example, anything you do to increase customer value can give you a competitive advantage.

Concentration—this is the foundation of all marketing success.

- If you are not a large-scale competitor, then focus on a segment, a niche, or a particle. Jelly Belly's particle market is flavors of jelly beans.
- Consider resegmenting the market. Finding smaller segments you can own will increase profitability.
- If price plays a key role, then the largest competitor can have the advantage of scale.
- A narrowly focused business will usually be more successful than one offering a broad variety. The general store is long gone—only the largest of the mass merchants survive.
- Consider offering a breadth of variety in your niche. For example, Staples promised to have any printer cartridge you need in stock.

Customer value—think value added.

- Increases in quality increase customer satisfaction and reduce costs over time.
- Providing better service or a better warranty is another component of customer satisfaction that increases the value perception.

Competitive advantage—think real differentiation.

- Finding a new distribution channel can relocate the battle-field.
- Introducing a new technology in the back of the house reduces costs in the front of the house. This can be a great differentiator.
- Find lower-cost sources.

Develop
a Plan
of Action

An army superior in strength takes action
like the bursting of pent-up waters
into a chasm of a thousand fathoms deep.

The elements of the art of war are:

1. *The measurement of space.*
2. *The estimation of quantities.*
3. *The calculation of figures.*
4. *Comparisons of strength.*
5. *Chances of victory.*

Measurements of space are derived from the ground. Quantities derive from measurement, figures from quantities, comparisons from figures and victory from comparisons.

Therefore, a victorious army is as one yi balanced against a grain, and a defeated army is as a grain balanced against one yi.

—Sun Tzu

"In every circle and truly at every table there are people who lead armies into Macedonia. These are great impediments to those who have the management of affairs."

—Quote from Roman general
(On wall in Gen. MacArthur's Tokyo office)

56

USE DATA TO PLAN FOR OVERWHELMING ADVANTAGES

The first rule of a marketing plan is that it must produce effective results. If efficiency were decisive, then surely accountants and administrators should decide all issues.

Too often we think we have plans when all we actually have are ideas in our head. Putting the plan down on paper establishes clarity and direction.

Marketing and sales must work together as a team to develop a plan that delivers the strategy. Problems arise when planning is separated from execution.

Gil Amelio, as Apple's CEO, set forth the following vectors:

- Create a clear vision of the future; invite contributions.
- Think of business as a value-delivery system.
- Focus on the intersection of what customers value and your core competencies.
- Define success clearly; identify critical success factors.
- Take bold initial steps. Communicate the direction.
- Identify sustainable competitive advantages.
- Realize that you cannot be number one in everything, but you must be number one in something.

A good test for determining whether the plan will really make a difference is to ask the question: What difference would it make if our competitors had a copy of our plan?

To write a plan, simply answer the questions Why? Who? What? When? Where? How?

Having the right product aimed at the right market is only part of the battle; being able to deliver the right product is the key issue.

A plan that is too sophisticated and rigid can take on a life of its own as it becomes "the way to win." The market is full of surprises. Allow for flexibility to adapt to changing situations.

You can expect a lot of help with your plans, more than you really need—or want.

Fight and Find Out

Agitate the enemy so as to ascertain his pattern of movement.
Lure him in the open so as to find out his vulnerable spots.
Probe him and learn
where his strength is abundant and deficient.

Therefore, if one knows the place and time of the coming battle, his troops can march a thousand li and fight on the field. But if one knows neither the spot nor the time, then one cannot manage to have the left wing help the right wing or the right wing help the left; the forces in the front will be unable to support the rear, and the rear will be unable to reinforce the front.

Although I estimate the troops of Yue as many, of what benefit is this superiority in terms of victory?

Thus, I say that victory can be achieved. For even if the enemy is numerically stronger, we can prevent him from fighting.

Therefore, analyze the enemy's battle plan, so as to have a clear understanding of its strong and weak points.

Now, the ultimate in disposing one's troops is to conceal them without ascertainable shape. In this way, the most penetrating spies cannot pry nor can the wise lay plans against you.

—Sun Tzu

LET THE MARKET TELL YOU WHAT TO DO

If you want to find out how the enemy is configured, "fight and find out," say the generals of history.

A test market is one of the most visible methods of inquiring into the nature of the market. A market test is a skirmish that offers the options of entering into battle or disengaging with minimal loss. Napoleon said, "The duty of the advance guard is to maneuver." So it is with test markets. You ignore the failures and exploit the successes.

Market testing is much like adjusting artillery fire. When the first round goes over the target, the next round is adjusted to fire short to attempt to bracket the target. Then you fire again. After a round lands on the target, you can "fire for effect." That is, you can roll out the program.

The marketing application of this process is that some testing may involve extreme situations. For example, if you think a low price is the critical element in achieving success, try a very low price. However, if you try testing by creeping down in price, you may need to run several tests in order to find out if a lower price will work. But if you tested with an extremely low price and got minimal results, abandon the effort. If the extremely low price test is a success, you now have a feel for the range within which adjustments can be made. That is, you abandon failures and continue to test successes.

I always advised my people never to report that a lower price, a better location, or some other element might have resulted in a successful test. The rule is to try the extremes that will make a test successful and adjust back to a profitable program. Think creatively—what different, effective actions can you take? Consider stealing conceptually from an entirely different business.

The mantra is "test-market, measure results, learn, adjust, and then test again." Soon you will know whether to proceed with a full rollout or to abandon the plan.

Do Not Underestimate

*He who lacks foresight
and underestimates his enemy
will surely be captured by him.*

In war, numbers alone confer no advantage. If one does not advance by force recklessly, and is able to concentrate his military power through a correct assessment of the enemy situation and enjoys full support of his men, that would suffice.

—Sun Tzu

A general in all of his projects should not only think so much about what he wishes to do as what his enemy will do; that he should never underestimate his enemy, but he should put himself in his place to appreciate difficulties and hindrances the enemy can interpose; that his plans will be deranged at the slightest even if has not foreseen everything and if he has not devised means with which to surmount obstacles.

—Frederick the Great
Instruction to His Generals, 1747

DO NOT REJECT NEW INFORMATION; CONSIDER YOUR WORST INDICATOR

Peter Drucker points out,

Professional management today sees itself in the role of a judge. . . . A top management that believes its job is to sit in judgment will inevitably veto the new idea.

We reject new information because it does not fit with our preconceived notions. Statisticians say that it takes eight data points to indicate a trend. In the human mind, it takes at least three to five observations before the average person will accept the new information. Stubborn people will take longer.

Admiral Rickover taught his nuclear submarine officers to "always believe your worst indicator." When a failure occurred at the Three Mile Island nuclear power plant, two of the indicators showed that everything was all right; one indicated a problem. Because the operators ignored their worst indicator, the system went critical. Eventually, disaster was avoided.

While one should not be too pessimistic, it's a good idea to thoroughly examine the underlying cause of your worst indicators. I have always liked to check my estimates using the "80 percent rule." That is, what will happen if I achieve only 80 percent of my planned success?

You may want to subject your plan to what the military calls a "murder board." That is, have it critically reviewed by a small group of people with knowledge of the situation.

Here is a simple model for evaluating competitive actions in order to determine options for action:

1. What is the strategic position of our competitor?
2. What actions has our competitor taken?
3. What have we done?
4. What do we expect our competitor to do?
5. What will we do?

Take Calculated Risks

*He orders his troops
for a decisive battle
and cuts off their return route,
as if he kicks away the ladder
behind the soldiers
when they have climbed up a height.*

When he leads his army deep into hostile territory, their momentum is trigger-released in battle. He drives his men now in one direction, then in another, like a shepherd driving a flock of sheep, and no one knows where he is going. To assemble the host of his army and bring it into danger—this may be termed the business of the general.

Set the troops to their tasks without revealing your designs. When the task is dangerous, do not tell them its advantageous aspect. Throw them into a perilous situation and they will survive; put them in desperate ground and they will live. For when the army is placed in such a situation, it can snatch victory from defeat.

—Sun Tzu

"Theory can give no formula with which to solve problems. It lets the mind take a look at objects and their relations and then the mind goes to the higher regions, there to act."

—Carl von Clausewitz
On War

ACTION
PRECEDES
VICTORY

Get out of the box. Travel down new roads. Choose unknown directions, and take that

great

mental

leap

in

the

dark.

Try something dramatically different. Ignore "the way we've always done it." Break through the division silos. Why did the army have to develop its own armed helicopters to provide close-in air support?" Because the Air Force was wedded to fighters and bombers.

We see the same problems in business. Departments who have first access to the new technology evaluate it in relation to their own mission. For example, when computerized reporting first became available, it was used for financial reports because that department originally controlled the technology.

In the military it is reconnaissance or a probing attack that generates the confidence to make a leap forward. Internally, it is how you get access to the newest business technology. Externally, it is how you learn the weakness of the opponent and how your own strength stacks up competitively.

Marketing creativity involves risk taking and can lead to extraordinary competitive advantage. It takes courage to be different and a lot of courage to be very different.

It can be riskier to be conventional than to be unconventional. What is revolutionary today is mundane tomorrow. Even the revolutionary Internet is about to lose the capital first letter and become merely the internet. (The telephone was once the Telephone.)

Before Panera Bread became the hot restaurant concept, it was the St. Louis Bread division of Au Bon Pain. Rebranded as Panera it became Au Bon Pain's primary growth vehicle, eventually causing Au Bon Pain to sell off its namesake business to focus only on Panera Bread.

"Unconventional wisdom" may be a better way to launch a new product or find a new market than conventional wisdom. Those who are first and successful often are able to define the market. Ted Turner took a risk when he launched a 24-hour news and information station in the 1970s. He did not copy the network news format; instead, he looked at the emerging trends of high interest in news and cable as a new technology. As a result, he created a powerful national brand—an opportunity that was missed by the networks, which were burdened with the baggage of sunk costs and the status quo.

Survival Drives Victory

In a desperate situation,
they fear nothing;
when there is no way out,
they stand firm.

Throw your soldiers into a position whence there is no escape, and they will choose death over desertion. For if prepared to die, how can the officers and men not exert their uttermost strength to fight? Deep in a hostile land they are bound together. If there is no help for it, they will fight hard.

Thus, without waiting to be marshaled, the soldiers will be constantly vigilant; without waiting to be asked, they will do your will; without restrictions, they will be faithful; without giving orders, they can be trusted.

Therefore, in dispersive ground, I would unify the determination of the army. In frontier ground, I would keep my forces closely linked. In key ground, I would hasten up my rear elements. In open ground, I would pay close attention to my defense. In focal ground, I would consolidate my alliances. In serious ground, I would ensure a continuous flow of provisions. In difficult ground, I would press on over the road. In encircled ground, I would block the points of access and egress. In desperate ground, I would make it evident that there is no chance of survival. For it is the nature of soldiers to resist when surrounded, to fight hard when there is no alternative, and to follow commands implicitly when they have fallen into danger.

—Sun Tzu

SURVIVAL IS THE ULTIMATE OBJECTIVE OF EVERY ENTERPRISE

If the "opportunity" doesn't destroy you; it will make you stronger.

We can learn much about survival from the guerrilla warrior. There is a similarity between the needs of the corporate guerrilla who must manage the success of a minor product line and those of the entrepreneurial guerrilla who manages a small business.

Although each may have a burning desire to succeed, motivation is not enough. The key to the guerrilla's strategy is being where the "elephant" isn't. Market share has no relevance.

Too often, the corporate guerrilla's superiors expect her or him to act like a gorilla—just like the big corporate brands. The corporate guerrilla's personal future lies in being recognized for her or his ability and finding opportunities elsewhere within the corporate structure. If your department closes down, circulate your résumé to other department heads. The small-business guerrilla who is not succeeding survives by moving to other brands, products, or markets. His or her customers are the small-business guerrilla's base of strength.

Successful guerrilla action often reverses the normal business practices. The guerrilla does not focus a major attack on a broad front; instead, he or she nibbles with multiple minor coups.

Here is the advice that Chairman Mao might have given to the guerrilla marketer:

- Capture smaller accounts first; get the big ones later.
- In every battle, find a point where you can have local superiority.
- Fight no battle without a plan for winning.

- Give way when under heavy attack. Find a new battle-ground, or a new war.
- Don't bunch up and depend on a single profit source. Keep your opportunities diversified.
- Service is one of your strengths.
- Plan personal reconnaissance. Know what's going on.
- Build your list of 10 sure things. When one opportunity is lost, you have nine more.

Fourth Principle
A Secure Position

The leader must take up a strong position,
inspire others to follow him, discover where
the enemy is weak and attack there.

—"The Precepts of Ssu Ma Jang Chu"
Fourth Century B.C.

> *STRATEGICALLY*
> A secure position establishes the basis for an offensive.
>
> *TACTICALLY*
> A secure position helps you make use of your natural strength.

Occupy a position that cannot easily be taken by your opponents.

THE MARKETPLACE

In general, the marketplace looks like this:

The Superpowers

The big ones in control.

The Secondary Powers

They play follow the leader or form an alliance.

The Business Guerrillas

Too small to be targeted, but always in danger.

The Superpowers

They own the territory, set the rules, and, like the 800-pound gorilla, sleep anywhere they want. The big dogs get the biggest pieces of meat.

The superpowers are in the protection business—they are as concerned with protecting their position on the high ground as they are with gaining new ground.

The superpowers get the largest market share because they *are* the superpowers. Microsoft owns the patents in computer operating systems and dominates the business applications software industry. Nabisco sells the most cookies because it has the most shelf space. McDonald's sells the most hamburgers because it has the most locations.

At the high ground, every day is combat day as the super-powers fight to keep out invaders. The defense is directed at attacking or terrorizing competitors so that they won't invade with new products.

Often the best defense is a continuing offensive, with brand extensions in different varieties and sizes.

Major competitors can emerge from outside the industry. The railroads' competition was the motor vehicle. Then buses lost business to airlines. The enemy of the typewriter was the computer.

The Secondary Powers

Their job is to get bigger so that they do not get smaller. They often achieve this by knocking off a lot of smaller companies rather than by attacking the major powers. It's easier to eliminate the weak than to attack the strong.

These secondary powers are in the vulnerable middle ground. They are facing attacks from both the big guys and the guerrillas. In the early emerging development of any industry, we see a normal distribution of big, midsize, and small companies. As the industry moves to maturity, the marketing action polarizes to the big at one extreme and the small specialists at the other. The never-never land where you never want to be is a medium-sized company in a mature industry.

The shakeout in retailing has almost demolished the medium-sized businesses. The small-town department store either has been wiped out or formed an alliance with a large chain. Flourishing at the two extremes are the giants and the boutiques.

The Guerrilla

In third place is everyone with a small market share, or a big share of a small market. These firms' biggest threat is the 800-pound gorilla.

Category killers in businesses such as toys, hardware, and office supplies have driven the smaller guerrillas out of business—and are in turn being threatened by the ultimate category killer, Wal-Mart.

Coca-Cola carefully watched the low-calorie and low-caffeine segments of the soft drink industry before jumping in with Diet Coke. The delay did not affect Coke's long-term success. While advantages like this can accrue to larger companies; smaller companies don't survive mistakes.

In computer hardware and software, Microsoft takes no prisoners.

The Positioning Cycle

In every industry, when a firm increases its market share, it creates serious problems for competitors as it erodes the competitors' base. This forces the competitors to compete for lesser positions that return ever-smaller profits. As market positions change, the one who captures the high ground gets the large amount of revenue, and all the accompanying advantages. Similarly, the loser's losses accumulate—negatively.

The Alliance

We see smaller organizations forming alliances with large organizations—often in the form of a franchise or licensing agreement. Here are two examples of giants entering into alliances:

- Send your FedEx package via the drop box at the local post office or Kinko's.
- Send funds via Western Union kiosks at your local chain supermarket.

These alliances prosper because they work for both customers and suppliers.

The partnership agreements so common in the auto industry can be a useful alliance for both producer and supplier in any industry.

Be
Invincible

*The skillful warriors in ancient times
first made themselves invincible
and then awaited
the enemy's moment of vulnerability.*

Invincibility depends on oneself, but the enemy's vulnerability on himself. It follows that those skilled in war can make themselves invincible but cannot cause an enemy to be certainly vulnerable. Therefore, it can be said that, one may know how to achieve victory, but cannot necessarily do so.

Invincibility lies in the defense; the possibility of victory in the attack. Defend yourself when the enemy's strength is abundant; and attack the enemy when it is inadequate.

Those who are skilled in defense hide themselves as under the most secret recesses of earth.

Those skilled in attack flash forth as from above the topmost heights of heaven.

Thus, they are capable both of protecting themselves and of gaining a complete victory.

Accordingly, a wise commander always ensures that his forces are put in an invincible position, and at the same time will be sure to miss no opportunity to defeat the enemy. . . . The commander adept in war enhances the moral influence and adheres to the laws and regulations. Thus it is in his power to control success.

—Sun Tzu

INVINCIBILITY LIES
IN THE DEFENSE;
THE POSSIBILITY OF VICTORY
IN THE ATTACK

In a memo to his War Cabinet, Winston Churchill wrote, "It is by devising new weapons, and above all by scientific leadership, that we shall cope with the enemy's superior power."

The franchise system offers opportunities for organizational strength. The failure rate of franchised organizations is much lower than that of independent businesses. Like the Greek phalanx, the franchise system has superiority in training and a united front.

The rules for achieving success with technology are: Be scrupulously objective and understand the limitations of the technology.

In the athletic shoe wars, Nike aims for the invincible high performance position. To reinforce its position, Nike maintains a staggering array of research and development facilities at its Beaverton, Oregon, campus: a running track with digital sensors, a basketball court with cameras at ankle height, a store of sample materials for future products, and a room that can create any weather condition. This attention to perfection of product performance is the essence of Nike's position.

Knowing that distribution channel selection can influence its image, Puma has chosen to avoid "discount" or "bargain" outlets. Puma is as interested in whom it does not sell to as in whom it does sell to.

New Balance is anti-Nike and anti-Puma in its search for an invincible position. New Balance sees a role in being different, and so it is "Endorsed by No One." Older folks like New Balance because it makes shoes for every foot width. New Balance's market share has been climbing steadily, and the company now has the number two position.

In the world of retailing, who is more invincible than Wal-Mart, with its goal of a 30 percent share of every business segment in which it participates? However, it is when you are on top and everything seems to be going all right, that you've really got to start worrying. You may not remember some who were on top such as Atari (the maker an early-generation of best-selling video games) or its strong competitor, Coleco. Grundig was a great name in radios and Bendix was on top for short time in automatic washers.

To be invincible, one must continually be on the attack.

Seize
Favorable
Positions

Take advantage of the enemy's unpreparedness.
Make your way by unexpected routes.
Attack him where he has taken no precautions.

In ancient times, those described as skilled in war knew how to make it impossible for the enemy to unite his van and his rear, for his large and small divisions to cooperate, for his officers and men to support each other, and for the higher and lower levels of the enemy to establish contact with each other.

When the enemy's forces were dispersed, they prevented him from assembling them; even when assembled, they managed to throw his forces into disorder. They moved forward when it was advantageous to do so; when not advantageous, they halted.

—Sun Tzu

PREEMPTIVE STRATEGIES

The preemptive strategy is a major action that secures a competitive advantage. You can do preemptive marketing with any elements of the marketing mix.

Walgreen's preemptive action has been to find the best locations. CEO David Bernauer says simply, "We have great real estate." Walgreen's has been concentrating on high-traffic corners for more than a decade. Competitors must initiate actions to compensate for Walgreen's location strength.

76

FIND
THE SWEET
SPOTS

It may surprise you to learn that vichyssoise is not of French origin. It was created at the New York Ritz-Carlton in 1917.

The idea that a foreign brand name has cachet was used by Reuben Mattus in 1959 when he innovated the Häagen-Dazs brand name. He knew that Americans thought that the rest of the world ate better than they did, and so would pay more for a foreign product. So, after years in the ice cream business, he created a richer, more expensive ice cream and made up a ridiculous, impossible-to-pronounce name. He even printed a map of Sweden on the carton. The rest is marketing history.

That doesn't mean that foreign is the only favorable position. Ben & Jerry's success is another legend at the unsophisticated end of the ice cream spectrum.

In a relatively short time, Starbucks has transformed one of the world's must commonplace beverages into a premium product. The carefully cultivated, widely recognized brand name extends far beyond the contents of the cup. Starbucks' growth can be attributed to its ability to position the product as a symbol. This positioning attracts repeat business without the expenditure of large amounts of money on advertising. According to one survey, the average customer visits Starbucks more than 15 times a month, and 10 percent visit twice a day!

The giants in the coffee business watched Starbucks occupy a premier position and steal market share. Now Starbucks is a lifestyle. Starbucks stores and kiosks are everywhere. Barnes & Noble serves it in its stores.

It is interesting how most of the distribution channel innovation comes from upstart competitors. Big companies that try to innovate new channels get stymied by their own culture.

Many startups succeed by defining their business in a manner that distinctly differentiates them from their competition. This differentiation can be in any area of business; it might be in distribution rather than manufacturing or service rather than sales.

Private hospitals secured a strong competitive position in some markets by getting both the best locations and the support of the best physicians. In the pizza wars, Pizza Hut established its strong brand position with location and advertising superiority. Domino's hasn't allowed anyone else to get a better position in the home delivery market.

Seek the Advantages of Natural Positions

*When an army takes up a position and sizes up
the enemy situation, it should pay attention to the following:*

- *When crossing the mountains, be sure to stay in the neighborhood of valleys.*
- *When encamping, select high ground facing the sunny side.*
- *When high ground is occupied by the enemy, do not ascend to attack.*

After crossing a river, you should get far away from it. When an advancing invader crosses a river, do not meet him in midstream. It is advantageous to allow half his force to get across and then strike.

In crossing salt marshes, your sole concern should be to get over them quickly, without any delay.

On level ground, take up an accessible position and deploy your main flanks on high grounds with the front lower than the back.

These are principles for encamping in the four situations named. By employing them, the Yellow Emperor conquered his four neighboring sovereigns.

—Sun Tzu

NATURAL FEATURES SUPPORT YOUR POSITION

We usually do not view a position as natural for an organization until the organization has occupied that position for some time. The most visible natural positions are at the high end and the low end.

What could be more natural then a carton of chocolate milk that screams the position of the Hershey brand? The brand name Disney signifies fun and entertainment.

At the high end of the retail spectrum are the Tiffany and Cartier positions where you expect to pay big money for any purchase. In luxury auto shopping, you expect good performance from the German Mercedes, the Japanese Lexus, or the American Cadillac or Lincoln.

Retailers such as Nordstrom's sell high-end brand names and provide outstanding service. When you visit one of Nordstrom's stores, you know that its service position is real. I've made a purchase and been welcomed by name when I returned several months later. Nordstrom's has more than the average number of salespeople in an industry where it's hard to get waited on. It provides all kinds of personal service to embellish its image.

The product and the brand have a major role in determining the natural position. It's easy to understand that a low-priced product in a category will have a low-end position and a high-priced product will have a high-end position. No one goes into the market with a low-quality, low-priced product and expects to stay very long—this is a nonposition position.

As Wal-Mart moved out in rural Arkansas selling to low-income customers, the store naturally adopted a low-price position. Any other position would be unnatural for their customers. To occupy the low price position, they need to have a low-cost distribution system. It is axiomatic that a low-price position can be occupied only if you are a low-cost operator.

Retailers adopt positions by branding their stores. No one expects to pay high prices in Big Lots or Dollar General stores. Those companies reinforce their position by advertising their low prices, and the perception is strengthened when you visit their stores.

Over time, you are who you naturally are. I was amused by the retailer at a conference who said, "Sometimes I don't believe my own ads." Neither did his customers.

Occupy the High Ground

In battle and maneuvering,
all armies prefer high ground to low,
and sunny places to shady. . . .

When you come to hills, dikes, or embankments, occupy the sunny side, with your main flank at the back. All these methods are advantageous to the army and can exploit the possibilities the ground offers.

If an army encamps close to water and grass with adequate supplies, it will be free from countless diseases and this will spell victory.

When heavy rain falls in the upper reaches of a river and foaming water descends, do not ford and wait until it subsides. When encountering "Precipitous Torrents," "Heavenly Wells," "Heavenly Prison," "Heavenly Net," "Heavenly Trap," and "Heavenly Cracks," you must march speedily away from them. Do not approach them. While we keep a distance from them we should draw the enemy toward them. We face them and cause the enemy to put his back to them.

If in the neighborhood of your camp there are dangerous defiles or ponds and low-lying ground overgrown with aquatic grass and reeds, or forested mountains with dense tangled undergrowth, they must be thoroughly searched, for these are possible places where ambushes are laid and spies are hidden.

—Sun Tzu

ALL ARMIES
PREFER HIGH GROUND
TO LOW

The importance of the moral high ground is better understood since the dot-com financial fiascos. On the first page of *The Art of War*, "moral influence" is listed as the first of five fundamental factors. Through the centuries, strategists have emphasized the importance of the strength that comes from having right on your side. Political and business empires have been built on the bedrock of moral strength.

Many successful organizations have a moral fervor in their mission. The more strongly this fervor permeates the organization, the greater is the strength of the offensive. The strength of belief that the organization's purpose is morally sound also strengthens the immunity to negative comments and bad publicity.

There is a long list of organizations that have succeeded because their people are dedicated to good business principles, and an equally long list of short-timers who are apparently dedicated to nothing. The physical act of "rallying around the flag" can do much to institutionalize the message. Many organizations actively organize events to generate enthusiasm and reinforce their core beliefs and values.

One business entrepreneur built a strong franchise for his product by making a "religion" of the company's dedication to protecting the profits of retailers in the distribution channel. His battle cry was guaranteed profits through carefully controlled retail pricing. While this posture has legal complications in today's business world, some organizations use selected distribution to minimize competition and assure the trade a more profitable product line. The privilege of belonging to this select group is the foundation for a fighting spirit. Col. Boyd in his lectures shared the following observations related to moral conflict:

- *Moral strength:* Mental capacity to overcome menace, uncertainty, and mistrust.
- *Moral values:* Human values that permit one to carry on in the face of menace, uncertainty, and defeat.
- *Moral victory:* Triumph of courage, confidence, and spirit (de corps) over fear, anxiety, and alienation when confronted by menace, uncertainty, and mistrust.
- *Moral authority:* Person or body that can give one the courage, confidence, and esprit to overcome menace, uncertainty, and mistrust.

"Conquesting" is a strategy for finding the high ground in a segment of the market. Most customers in these markets have already been claimed by competitors. This is most visible in the auto industry, where market share must be "conquested" from competitors. New models such as the minivan and the SUV were introduced to minimize cannibalizing and maximize conquests of new customers.

The Best Defense Is to Plan a Good Offense

It is a doctrine of war that we must not rely on the likelihood of the enemy not coming, but on our own readiness to meet him; not on the chance of his not attacking, but on the fact that we have made our position invincible.

What can subdue the hostile neighboring rulers is to hit what hurts them most; what can keep them constantly occupied is to make trouble for them; and what can make them rush about is to offer them ostensible allurements.

—Sun Tzu

"A passive defense is deadly, and does not win battles. Aggressive action is safer and more prolific of victory. Troops that have the initiative, hold the advantage. They force others to play their game."

—Lincoln C. Andrews
Tactical Rules, 1916

OFFENSIVE THINKING AND ACTION BREEDS VICTORY

Napoleon said, "Defensive war does not exclude attacking, just as offensive war does not exclude defending." When you are constantly on the defensive, you seldom win. If you stop the enemy attack, there will most likely be another one.

Much of the success of American industry has been the result of an internally focused and less visible defense centered on productivity and higher quality. The strength of this defense is that it provides a strong offensive capability.

An investment in quality systems can be a good defense. The net result is that product performance improves and costs go down. When world-class quality is achieved, not only has the organization designed a protection against foreign invasions, but from this secure base it can launch world-competitive products.

The marketing rule is that you must have quality in every detail—in people, products, and programs. Considering the fragility of the human element, you do not allow your plan to fail because of any controllable physical elements such as product quality, performance specifications, or delivery time.

Harley-Davidson was in big trouble fighting against the legions of foreign motorcycle importers. It restructured its operations to focus on quality and earned a strong position in the market.

Novartis, the name given to the merger of Sandoz and Ciba-Geigy in pharmaceuticals, secured a sound defense with a $250 million expenditure for a new research and development facility.

Attacking yourself can be the best defense. Those who do not do so are doomed to oblivion. If you don't innovate, your competitor will. Gillette does it with every new razor. Intel attacks itself with every new chip. Microsoft is its own best competitor with newer versions of software. Heinz attacked itself when it abandoned the famous glass ketchup bottle and innovated a new plastic squeeze bottle.

Years ago, KFC found that attacking lunch was better than attacking hamburgers—building its own non-supper business was the best way to defend against the hamburger chains.

Fifth Principle
Offensive Action

A great army must be consolidated,
big forces must be well exercised,
the most suitable control must be chosen,
and the army must be ready to take advantage
of opportunities.

This is what is called being prepared.

—"The Precepts of Ssu Ma Jang Chu"
Fourth Century B.C.

> ### STRATEGICALLY
> Offensive action provides initiative of movement.
>
> ### TACTICALLY
> Offensive action keeps you in control.

Keep on the offensive to secure freedom of action.

 Planning is important; however, successful execution of the plan is critical to success. Only offensive action achieves decisive results. Action permits the manager to exploit the initiative and impose his or her will on the marketplace or the competition. Key to the successful offense are skill, preparation, training, and, above all, information. History proves that a successful attack is won before it begins. The norm is the confusion of not enough time, not enough resources, and not enough information.

Only rarely will exact details be known. While the attempt to get more information is made as a matter of course, waiting for news in a difficult situation is a bad error.

When companies leave market segments open, competition moves into these segments. Then a great deal of money must be expended to earn back market share.

The offensive spirit must permeate the company.

INNOVATION OFFENSIVE

Ford's innovation in mass production offered the opportunity to reduce prices, and cars were sold to people who would not otherwise have bought a new auto. This is great marketing.

At General Motors, Alfred Sloan segmented the market, offering different lines of cars for people who represented different demographics. This is also great marketing.

Sloan's segmentation won over Ford's "any color as long as it's black" Model T strategy—and the marketing battle rages on.

Innovation is not confined to physical products; you can innovate in any area of the marketing spectrum. Time after time, the innovation offensive wins the day. Here are a few basics to keep in mind as you consider launching the innovation offensive:

Keep it simple. The simple works best.
Be focused. Fill a specific need.
Start small. Then you can correct as you go along.
Build on strengths. You are already doing what you do best.
Be in sync with the market. You want to sell it now.

The offensive must be at a time and place of your own choosing. The Roman Vegetius said, "It is the nature of war that what is beneficial to you is detrimental to the enemy and what is of service to him always hurts you. It is therefore a maxim never to do, or to omit doing, anything as a consequence of his actions, but to consult invariably your own interest only." Napoleon said, "A well-established maxim of war is not to do anything which your enemy wishes—and for the single reason that he so wishes."

Beware: The offensive does not offer a solution to all problems. Your desire for offensive action must be matched by wisdom. You have probably never heard of a Roman consul named Varro. His public promise was that he would attack the enemy wherever and whenever he found them. At the first opportunity, he charged out of camp—and into disaster. He was a loser.

The best way to win in marketing is to take the offensive, and if you are forced to assume the defensive, it must only be a temporary position. The offensive provides the most powerful means of marshaling the corporate resources and bringing them into action. The very fact that the offensive requires more activity than trying to maintain the status quo is in its favor. Between any two competitors, other things being equal, the more active will prevail.

The first rule of marketing must be to seize the offensive and permanently retain the initiative. Grasp the customer's attention and stay focused on improving the relationship. It is a maxim to never voluntarily surrender the initiative.

Markets are changing at a fast pace. The marketing management task extends well beyond promoting existing products and services. The marketing initiative is one of continually creating new opportunities. This can involve finding new customers, building new alliances, improving logistics, adding new features and benefits, and more. The ultimate goal is always to build long-term relationships.

ORGANIZING THE OFFENSIVE

The following three key components are basic to the marketing offensive:

1. *A focal point.* A critical mass must be focused. Put yourself in your competitor's shoes. How would he attack the market? This tells you how to organize your own attack.
2. *Shock.* It is generated by mobility and speed. Keep moving. You are most vulnerable when standing still—not when actively finding new ways to serve customers.
3. *Pursuit.* When something works, keep on using it. Multiply your successes. Abandon your failures. Repetition and consistency of message are important components of marketing.

Marshall Adequate Resources

One who begrudges
the expenditure of one hundred pieces of gold
and remains ignorant of the enemy's situation
is completely devoid of humanity.

Such a man is no leader of the troops; no capable assistant to his sovereign; no master of victory.

Generally, when an army of one hundred thousand is raised and dispatched on a distant war, the expenses borne by the people together with the disbursements made by the treasury will amount to a thousand pieces of gold per day.

There will be continuous commotion both at home and abroad; people will be involved with convoys and exhausted from performing transportation services, and seven hundred thousand households will be unable to continue their farmwork.

—Sun Tzu

DETERMINE YOUR PRIORITIES

You must decide what level of mind share can be attained with each customer group in the distribution channel. Then allocate financial resources to achieve those objectives.

Comparative levels of mind share are

1. *Awareness.* Establish a beachhead. The customer group knows that your product or service exists.
2. *Acceptance.* Penetration of mind share. The customer group would consider purchasing your product or service.
3. *Preference.* Occupation of mind share. The customer group prefers your product or service.

Of course, one would like to be the brand of preference for every customer; however, I've never had enough funds to achieve this lofty objective.

This simple matrix can help organize priorities. Here is how expenditures might look if you are going to push the product through trade channels:

Mind Share	Sales Force	Middleman	End Customer
Awareness			$
Acceptance		$$	
Preference	$$$		

At the opposite extreme, if you are going to pull the product through trade channels, your resources would be allocated in the following manner:

Mind Share	Sales Force	Middleman	End Customer
Awareness	$		
Acceptance		$$	
Preference			$$$

Make a decision and allocate your resources.

Seize the Initiative

*He who occupies the field of battle first
and awaits his enemy is at ease;
he who arrives later
and joins battle in haste is weary.*

*And, therefore, one skilled in war
brings the enemy to the field of battle
and is not brought there by him.*

One able to make the enemy come of his own accord does so by offering him some advantage. And one able to stop him from coming does so by inflicting damage on him.

Therefore, on the day the decision is made to launch war, you should close the passes, destroy the official tallies, and stop the passage of all emissaries. Examine the plan closely in the temple council and make final arrangements.

If the enemy leaves a door open, you must rush in. Seize the place the enemy values without making an appointment for battle with him. Be flexible and decide your line of action according to the situation on the enemy side.

At first, then, exhibit the coyness of a maiden until the enemy gives you an opening; afterwards be swift as a running hare, and it will be too late for the enemy to oppose you.

—Sun Tzu

"Seizing the offensive is the only strategy that can work in an expanding and competitive economy—regardless of whether it is national or international. U.S. business must take the initiative internationally, in price, in styling, in innovation and design, and in marketing. We have

to accept what we all know to be elemental—that taking a defensive position can, at best, only limit losses. And we need gains."

—Peter Drucker

TAKING ACTION MAKES YOU MASTER OF THE SITUATION

The most effective and decisive way to reach the objective is to seize, maintain, and exploit the initiative. Being on the offensive puts you in control of your relationship with your customers and forces your competitors to react.

Either you spend time preparing extensive plans or you set goals and get going. It would seem that the choice is often between doing more preparation or doing it now. The marketing manager must find that careful balance between getting ready and getting going. The greatest odds for success lie on the side of action.

For decades, Campbell's only meaningful entry into the soup category was its dominant red-and-white can of condensed soup. Then Progresso snatched the initiative with good-tasting soups that did not need to be mixed with water. Campbell's responded by moving to the initiative. It took a stew that wasn't selling well and called it chunky soup. Then it improved the convenience of its soups with microwaveable packages and pull-top cans. The battle continues.

The offensive originates in the mind of the marketing general and then becomes a physical act. Stay in the office for a week and you'll find enough problems originating in the bureaucracy to stay in the office for another week. Spend a week in the field and you'll need to spend another. Both office and field activities offer opportunities for thinking about initiatives. However, there is a real difference between the orientation and results from office-generated and field-inspired initiatives.

Enable Momentum

When torrential water tosses boulders,
it is because of momentum.

Therefore, a skilled commander sets great store by using the situation to the best advantage, and does not make excessive demands on his subordinates. Hence he is able to select the right men and exploits the situation. He who takes advantage of the situation uses his men in fighting as rolling logs or rocks. It is the nature of logs and rocks to stay stationary on the flat ground, and to roll forward on a slope. If four-cornered, they stop; if round-shaped, they roll. Thus, the energy of troops skillfully commanded is just like the momentum of round rocks quickly tumbling down from a mountain thousands of feet in height. This is what "use of energy" means.

—Sun Tzu

GET MOMENTUM GOING

The conventional wisdom in football coaching is that a team can control the tempo of the game by controlling three time periods:

The first five minutes of the game
The last five minutes of the first half
The last five minutes of the second half

In these crucial time periods a team can gain or lose momentum.

STRIVE FOR
THE CONTINUOUS
ATTACK

Offensive action must be a continuing process. Only then does it permit you to maintain freedom of action, meet unexpected developments, and determine the course of the marketing battle.

Every great commander of every age has longed for the continuous attack because as long as momentum is maintained, the unit is winning.

The world is full of "enablers" that help sell products. The premium with the purchase and coupons are enablers that help new products get off the ground and established products gain momentum. A different package concept can be an enabler.

The author was involved in the marketing of the first video game. Sales were slow. The term *video game* had no meaning until an electronic Ping-Pong game named Pong appeared in airports. The coin-operated game served as an enabler—that is, it created the interest that enabled sales to gain momentum.

Retailers and wholesalers alike gain momentum with special sales events and limited-time offers. What's important is to get started and then find ways to gain momentum.

Newell Corporation is enabling momentum by putting power on the front lines. It uses squads of field representatives to get its Rubbermaid and Sharpie products prominently displayed by key retailers.

When Miller Brewing Company rolled its Lite beer into test markets in 1973, it had no idea that the brew would inspire legions of products named "light" or "lite." Lite is an invented word that Miller acquired from another brewer. The right product at the right time creates its own momentum. The copies by competitors generate more momentum.

The lesson to be learned from the failures in war and marketing is that a once-successful formula must constantly be reevaluated; otherwise, with time, it may become a liability. If you aren't carefully listening to the beat of the market, your customers will drift away—and then your lack of sales tells all.

Go for a Breakthrough

Use the normal force to engage.
Use the extraordinary to win.

That the whole army can sustain the enemy's all-out attack without suffering defeat is due to operations of extraordinary and normal forces. Troops thrown against the enemy as a grindstone against eggs is an example of the strong beating the weak.

Generally, in battle, now, to a commander adept at the use of extraordinary forces, his resources are as infinite as the heaven and earth, as inexhaustible as the flow of the running rivers. They end and begin again like the motions of the sun and moon. They die away and then are reborn like the changing of the four seasons.

There are not more than five musical notes, but the various combinations of the five notes bring about more melodies than can ever be heard.

There are not more than five basic pigments, yet in blending them together it is possible to produce more colors than can ever be seen.

There are not more than five cardinal tastes, but the mixture of the five yields more flavors than can ever be tasted.

In battle, there are not more than two kinds of postures—operation of the extraordinary force and operation of the normal force, but their combinations give rise to an endless series of maneuvers. For these two forces are mutually reproductive. It is like moving in circles, never coming to an end. Who can exhaust the possibilities of their combinations?

—Sun Tzu

USE THE NORMAL TO ENGAGE, THE EXTRAORDINARY TO WIN

You achieve a marketing breakthrough by applying the combined force of several principles. Strategists use the appropriate term *force multipliers* to describe this cumulative application.

As you add the power of additional principles, each additional principle has a multiplier effect. It's not $2 + 2 + 2 + 2 = 8$, but rather $2 \times 2 \times 2 \times 2 = 16$.

In the battles of marketing, it is difficult to consider the principle of Maneuver independent of Concentration of Resources because maneuver is the thought process that shapes how we concentrate our resources. With good Intelligence systems, we will concentrate in the right place, and Offensive Action will release the energy. This is how you organize multiple principles in mutually supportive roles.

The problem is that your competitor is trying to win in the same engagement. By taking Sun Tzu's advice about using the extraordinary to win, you get the breakthrough.

For example, don't just think about having a great display at a trade show, go to the extraordinary extreme of thinking how your display can be so unique that you "own the show"—that is, you own all of the attention at the trade show. I've done this by stacking up a million dollars in one-dollar bills to dramatize a profit opportunity and by giving away 6-foot-high stuffed pink panthers with an order for a pink panther video game.

Everybody throws away direct-mail pieces, but receiving food in the mail is extraordinary. No one throws food away. I've used a jar of honey to remind customers that we could sweeten up their profits, a jar of pear jam to announce a new product that came in "pairs," and a box of breakfast cereal with an ad for our product on the back as a reminder of the advertising campaign.

When I wanted a return reply, I sent the batteries for a free radio that would be provided when we received the return reply card. Only the tax collector gets a better return then we did on that mailing.

To gain a breakthrough, you must do the unusual. This does not guarantee success, but it gives you the best chance of success.

Have
Tactical Flexibility

---

*Tactics change
in an infinite variety of ways
to suit changes in the circumstances.*

Even though we show people the victory gained by using flexible tactics in conformity to the changing situations, they do not comprehend this. People all know the tactics by which we achieved victory, but they do not know how the tactics were applied in the situation to defeat the enemy. Hence no one victory is gained in the same manner as another.

Hence, there are neither fixed postures nor constant tactics in warfare. He who can modify his tactics in accordance with the enemy situation and thereby succeeds in winning may be said to be divine. Of the five elements, none is ever predominant; of the four seasons, none lasts forever; of the days, some are longer and others shorter, and of the moon, it sometimes waxes and sometimes wanes.

—Sun Tzu

"Military officials say no single, decisive moment tipped the scales [in the Iraq War]. The strategy—devised to exploit enemy weakness and to capitalize on American strengths in weapons technology, communications, surveillance, and maneuvering—emphasized flexibility above all else. Battlefield commanders were encouraged to improvise in a way that some compared to a quarterback calling audibles at the line of scrimmage."

—*New York Times*, Apr. 13, 2003

FIFTH PRINCIPLE

NO ONE VICTORY
IS GAINED IN THE
SAME MANNER AS ANOTHER

While strategies remain constant, tactics must be adapted to each new situation. The battle for market share is much like a tug of war. As each side exercises power, the other reacts with an offsetting force. The result is a standoff.

When you have failed to achieve your objective, the mere reinforcement of weight is not enough. If you have strengthened yourself, it is probable that your competitors will also have strengthened themselves. In addition, their success in repulsing you may also have strengthened their morale.

"More, better, faster" is not a new tactic. The organization must go back to the drawing board to examine the tactics—the contact components. You must go through the entire marketing mix to determine what is working and what is not working.

The Roman Empire found that a combination of speed and mobility gave it both offensive and defensive flexibility. Roman troops could march 30 miles a day on an extensive network of all-weather roads. Legions could be quickly shuffled around the empire to respond as needed. This network gave Rome more flexibility in offense and defense.

It's easy to make changes. What is difficult is making the right changes. I've seen promotions that were mediocre the first year achieve remarkable success the next year. The problem was not the event, but rather the change to a new event. The second time around, everyone had a much better understanding of how to play their position. The fast-food restaurant business is all about the right combination of quality, value, service, and cleanliness—QVSC is their mantra. Miss on any one component and the business goes down. Wendy's stresses variety. Taco Bell goes for the low-price position. McDonald's aims for consistent quality.

Nestlé is trying to maneuver Kit Kat into position as the alternative to the competitive Mars bar (the world's most popular candy). Local flexibility is key. Kit Kat's formula is different almost everywhere. The Russian version is coarser than the German version and not as sweet. Each product variation is the result of local market research. Says former marketing executive and now chief executive Peter Brabeck, "There is no global consumer for the food-and-beverage business."

Plan a
Speedy Victory

While we have heard of stupid haste in war,
we have not yet seen
a clever operation that was prolonged.

In directing such an enormous army, a speedy victory is the main object.

If the war is long delayed, the men's weapons will be blunted and their ardor will be dampened. If the army attacks cities, their strength will be exhausted. Again, if the army engages in protracted campaigns, the resources of the state will not suffice. Now, when your weapons are blunted, your ardor dampened, your strength exhausted and your treasure spent, neighboring rulers will take advantage of your distress to act. In this case, no man, however wise, is able to avert the disastrous consequences that ensue.

There has never been a case in which a prolonged war has benefited a country. Therefore, only those who understand the dangers inherent in employing troops know how to conduct war in the most profitable way.

Hence, what is valued in war is a quick victory, not prolonged operations.

—Sun Tzu

LOGISTICAL
MOBILITY WINS

While Napoleon's opponents marched at the orthodox 70 paces per minute, the French marched at the faster rate of 120 paces per minute, a rate almost twice as fast. Think of the competitive advantage that can accrue from being able to move twice as fast as your competition.

THE POSITIVE CONSEQUENCES OF SPEED ACCRUE TO THE OFFENSIVE

In China, Ting Hsin International dominated the new instant-noodle market 5 years after opening its first factory. The second-oldest brother in this family company describes his success in a series of mottos: "Dare to try." "Grab your chance." "Move ahead."

Opening new locations in new geographic areas is the way many merchants plan for speedy growth. Papa John's moved to a lead position in the pizza wars by rapidly expanding to new locations. By opening 13,000 storefronts in 60 countries, Subway rapidly moved into a top position in the sub sandwich market.

New retail locations are extensively publicized in an effort to rapidly attract new customers. "Grand openings" emphasize

1. *Price:* Free is one of the most powerful words in the English language. Retailers use word "free" to gain a speedy short-term increase in new customers who will return often.
2. *Events:* At a store opening of the first Best Buy in a new metropolitan area, families lined up inside the store. Why? Spiderman was there in person with glossy photos to be signed. Kids were clutching Spiderman comic books and plush dolls—all awaiting the "authentic" signature.
3. *Education:* Providing information on products and services attracts people with special interests. At a recent grand opening of a Weis Markets grocery in Pennsylvania, the major attraction was a giant fresh swordfish. Customers were shown how the fish is cut into steaks for cooking.

Time can be your worst enemy and your best ally:

- The later you start, the more time you require.
- If you wait for approval from headquarters, you are too late.
- Rapid decision making produces rapid action.
- Delayed decisions inevitably lose their positive quality.

Sixth Principle
Surprise

If you take a few men
and make a sudden surprise attack
on a narrow road
with loud sounding of gongs
and drums,
the biggest army may be thrown into confusion.

—"Wu Chi on *The Art of War*"
Fourth Century B.C.

> **STRATEGICALLY**
> Surprise requires skillful planning.
>
> **TACTICALLY**
> Surprise occurs when it is too late for your opponent to react.

Surprise is the best way to gain psychological dominance and deny the initiative to your opponent.

 A military text says, "Strike first and unexpectedly, attain surprise in strength, point of attack, and through treachery."

THE MARKETING SURPRISE

Surprise in marketing will have a different configuration. Physically and psychologically, surprise denies your competitor the initiative by allowing you to strike at a time or place where he or she is unprepared. It is not essential that your competitor be taken totally unaware, but only that the competitor becomes aware too late to react effectively.

Surprise in marketing occurs most often when companies do not take new competition seriously. In the business arena, surprise is most often not an event but rather the result of recognizing that something undesirable has been happening.

Business strategist Bruce Henderson (founder of the Boston Consulting Group) says that if you want to achieve surprise, you do things your competitor will not see as a threat—such as entering the market in a segment where you do not compete directly. (It helps if you have chosen to enter a rapidly growing segment of the market.) As you grow in size and expand into adjacent segments, you eventually become a threat. When outside observers look back, it looks as if the new entrant was smarter—actually surprise was achieved by building from a nonthreatening position.

What American auto manufacturer saw the Japanese entry into the small-car segment of the auto industry as a threat? What retailer viewed Wal-Mart as a threat during its early years? It was years later that competitors were surprised.

Surprise can decisively shift the balance of power and achieve success out of proportion to the efforts.

SECRECY IS A PARTNER OF SURPRISE

It's not difficult to recall military battles in which secrecy played a major role in achieving surprise. In the Gulf War, the combined forces moved offensive units laterally along the front line to a point where they could drive deeply into Iraq unopposed. In the Battle of the Bulge, the Germans secretly moved a large force many miles. In the Korean War, the United Nations forces were unaware of the large armies the Chinese had moved into North Korea.

The marketing application of the silent attack can be found in small, privately held companies and large corporations that grow their own management structure. In these organizations, marketing secrecy is easier to maintain than in companies with a more mobile management staff.

Marketers who use secrecy as a major ingredient of surprise don't talk about it. Secrecy surrounds Nordstrom's department stores, where executives are reluctant to talk about the company's accomplishments or mode of operations. Like a military force planning an invasion, Southwest Airlines never announces a new destination before it actually enters the market. It doesn't want to give competitors time to launch a counterattack. To camouflage its intentions, it even lists "decoy airports" in talks with analysts.

In Lima, Peru, officials of the Phillips Company successfully countered the planned competitive introduction of a new high-tech product. When they found out on Wednesday that a competitor was planning to advertise a prototype on Sunday, they flew in their own prototype for a Saturday press conference. As a result, their new product ended up as "news" in the same Sunday paper as their competitor's ad.

In launching a new product, there is always a tendency to dribble the information into the market. A small announcement now, a comment later, and by the time the product gets to market, too many competitors have figured out how to blunt the threat.

At the British disaster at Gallipoli, evidence shows that the British would have been successful if they had used at the outset even a fair proportion of the forces they ultimately expended. By parceling out their forces, they lost the element of surprise and then the opportunity to achieve superiority.

Plan
Surprise

Launch the attack where he is unprepared;
take action when it is unexpected.

All warfare is based on deception. Therefore, when able to attack, we must pretend to be unable; when employing our forces, we must seem inactive; when we are near, we must make the enemy believe we are far away; when far away, we must make him believe we are near.

Offer a bait to allure the enemy, when he covets small advantages; strike the enemy when he is in disorder. If he is well prepared with substantial strength, take double precautions against him. If he is powerful in action, evade him. If he is angry, seek to discourage him. If he appears humble, make him arrogant. If his forces have taken a good rest, wear them down. If his forces are united, divide them.

These are the keys to victory for a strategist. However, it is impossible to formulate them in detail beforehand.

He changes his arrangements and alters his plans in order to make others unable to see through his strategies. He shifts his campsites and undertakes marches by devious routes so as to make it impossible for others to anticipate his objective.

—Sun Tzu

"Inaction leads to surprise, and surprise to defeat, which is after all only a form of surprise."

—Ferdinand Foch
Precepts, 1919

A SURPRISE MOVE
CAN SHIFT
THE BALANCE OF POWER

Once upon a time, Lever Brothers was the big winner in the laundry and toothpaste wars. Then Procter & Gamble launched Tide as the first synthetic laundry detergent and Crest as a cavity fighter. As households moved away from wringer-type washers, they found a box of Tide in their new automatic washer. The American Dental Society's endorsement of Crest left Lever Brothers in the lurch. Both moves were typical of marketing surprises—the competitor became aware of the action too late to react effectively and was forced into a defensive mode.

A Lever Brothers alumnus says, "It was difficult to reinvest in R&D, marketing, and plant modernization. All that stuff feeds on itself. The fat cats get fatter and the others get skinnier." Another former executive says that the beating Lever Brothers took from P&G created "a lurking lack of confidence. . . . The company's executives were always trying to play catch-up and an inferiority complex permeated decision making." Once the initiative is lost, it is hard to regain.

Now Procter & Gamble's prime products are under attack from Colgate and Kimberly Clark. P&G knew that Colgate's Total was coming to market as the only toothpaste approved by the FDA to fight gingivitis—but it wasn't concerned. It should have been, because Total leap-frogged Crest to eventually became number one in every country in the world.

For years, P&G was in the business of creating surprise with new products and acquisitions. Then it fell into the business of managing surprises.

The transfer of marketing control from power producers to power retailers is a problem facing all manufacturers. When power retailers introduce their own brands, the power producers are not exactly surprised, but the loss of sales is costly.

Generate the Mismatch

*When the strike of a hawk breaks the body of its prey,
it is because of timing.*

Thus, in battle, a good commander creates a posture releasing an irresistible and overwhelming momentum, and his attack is precisely timed in a quick tempo. The energy is similar to a fully drawn crossbow; the timing, the release of the trigger. Amid turmoil and tumult of battle, there may be seeming disorder and yet no real disorder in one's own troops. In the midst of confusion and chaos, your troops appear to be milling about in circles, yet it is proof against defeat.

—Sun Tzu

"Create tangles of threatening events and repeatedly generate mismatches. Disorient his mind. Disrupt his operations. Overload his system.

Get inside your adversary's observation–orientation–decision–action loops (at all levels) by being more subtle, indistinct, irregular and quicker—yet appear to be otherwise.

Stretch out opponent's time to respond while compressing our own response time."

— Col. John Boyd
Lecture Notes

INITIATE THE OBSERVATION–ORIENTATION–DECISION–ACTION TIME CYCLE

In new product development, it takes more than the accepted basics of high quality, low cost, and differentiation to succeed in today's world markets. The new rules add speed and flexibility as key components in moving products to market.

In the war in Iraq, information on the whereabouts of Saddam Hussein triggered the first attack. This rapid maneuver is an approach fostered by Colonel Boyd, who defined it as a fighter pilot. Boyd's belief is that success involves the use of maneuver, surprise, deception, and speed to find an opponent's weakness.

Fighter pilots stress the importance of "getting inside" in a dogfight by turning and maneuvering more quickly than the enemy so you can fix your guns on the opponent's plane before the opponent knows what you are doing.

You must knock your opponent off balance with fast, unpredictable tactics that will surprise and confuse her or him. By the time your adversary observes what you are doing, orients to it, decides what to do, and takes action, it will be too late. Boyd calls this cycle the observation–orientation–decision–action (OODA) loop.

The key to victory, says Boyd, is to generate the mismatch by operating at a faster tempo than your opponent.

The marketing application is to figure out how to move faster than your competitor. This requires hard-hitting marketing attacks aimed at your competitor. You generate the mismatch when you are in position in the market before your competitor can comprehend what is taking place. You see this in the rapid rollout of new products, with competitors scrambling to react. It's when the largest companies bring out new technology that we have the biggest dysfunction in the marketplace, because the giants have the resources to make an impact.

Moving at a faster tempo requires good information about your customers. Being prepared with knowledge gives you the confidence to move nimbly and rapidly when opportunities arise.

To achieve surprise, marketing forces must move rapidly. Speed and caution are opposite sides of the same coin. You can never have both caution and speed. Tactical surprise is usually the result of the daring, the imaginative, and the ingenious. It will rarely be gained by recourse to the obvious.

Keep Your Opponent Confused

Against those skillful in attack,
the enemy does not know where to defend.

Against the experts in defense,
the enemy does not know where to attack.

Thus, when the enemy is at ease, he is able to tire him; when well fed, to starve him; when at rest, to make him move. All these can be done because you appear at points which the enemy must hasten to defend.

That you may march a thousand li without tiring yourself is because you travel where there is no enemy.

That you are certain to take what you attack is because you attack a place the enemy does not or cannot protect.

That you are certain of success in holding what you defend is because you defend a place the enemy must hasten to attack.

How subtle and insubstantial that the expert leaves no trace. How divinely mysterious that he is inaudible. Thus, he is master of his enemy's fate.

His offensive will be irresistible if he plunges into the enemy's weak points; he cannot be overtaken when he withdraws if he moves swiftly. Hence, if we wish to fight, the enemy will be compelled to an engagement even though he is safe behind high ramparts and deep ditches. This is because we attack a position he must relieve.

If we do not wish to fight, we can prevent him from engaging us even though the lines of our encampment be merely traced out on the ground. This is because we divert him from going where he wishes.

—Sun Tzu

SOME ACTIONS
REQUIRE STEALTH
AND DECEPTION

Blend subtlety and secrecy to keep the opponent confused so that she or he knows neither where to attack nor where to defend.

The secrecy in many companies prior to a trade show could be a model for national security. Price sheets are printed at the last minute. Products to be displayed are kept under wraps. Private showrooms at nearby hotels are rented for the newest secret "weapons." Customers are admitted to these showrooms "by invitation only."

I can recall a trade show where a competitor announced a new home computer that would retail at an unbelievably low price point. The product was on display in a glass case that could be viewed only from several feet away. The company's previous success in introducing unique new products added to the belief that this new computer was real. Fearing this new product, several potential entrants withdrew from the market. Later, when competitors began to realize that the product would not materialize, it was too late to react in time for the prime selling season. It was a move right out of Colonel Boyd's lectures on the OODA loop, when he said, "Shape or influence events so that we not only magnify our spirit and strength but also negatively influence potential adversaries."

Direct-mail tests have the advantage of secrecy. The private sale that's advertised to customers only by direct mail is a way to reduce competitors' knowledge and reaction. In any direct-mail test, you can mail out a small number to gauge the response. Depending on the profit projections, you can then either stage a full rollout or abandon the project. It's all done quietly. Rarely will your competitors know what is going on.

Market-test your programs in geographic areas or channels of distribution, such as military commissaries, that your competition does not closely monitor.

To confuse your opponent, think about the kind of attack a guerrilla might launch, or plan a blitz effort in a critical segment of the market.

Be Disruptive
and Intrusive

*Those who use fire to assist their attacks can
achieve tangible results.
When the force of the flames has reached its height,
follow it up with an attack.
Those who use inundations can make their attacks
more powerful.*
—Sun Tzu

MERCHANDISING GETS ATTENTION

While it is the responsibility of the marketing manager to
develop the right product and plan (strategy) and it is the responsibility of the sales manager to marry the product and the customer (tactics), more is required. The promotional link between
marketing and selling is called merchandising. In retail organizations, merchandising is a major function of the marketing manager. Merchandising is all the things you do to get favorable
attention for your product.

The term *merchandising* is most often found in retailing where
"merchandise selections" are made and "merchandising dis-
plays" are designed.

DISRUPT THE MIND
AND INTRUDE
INTO THAT DISRUPTION

Generals say that if you want to win, you must dislocate the
enemy and exploit that dislocation.

The marketing equivalent is to be

DIS RUP TIVE
and
INTRUSIVE

That is, the implementation of your marketing effort must be staged to disrupt the customer's mind and intrude into that disruption with the benefits of your product or service. Your way of differentiating yourself from the pack should be energetic and "in good taste"—not obnoxious.

The opportunities for intrusive and disruptive marketing campaigns are endless—and so are the results. In order to succeed, the action must tie into the product in some memorable way. For example,

- When we stacked up a million dollars in one-dollar bills at a trade show, we were dramatizing a profit opportunity.
- When Federal Express delivered 30,000 coffee cakes on a Saturday morning, it was touting its new Saturday delivery.
- When Araldite glued a car body to a billboard in England, it was promoting its brand of glue.

The retailer who advertised snowblowers in early summer was being disruptive and intrusive. He got a lot of attention and was mentioned on TV news programs. Two weeks later, when he advertised lawn mowers, a lot of people knew who he was.

Sometimes, even little things can make a big difference. An old-fashioned popcorn popper can draw a crowd at a trade show. The aroma gets people off the aisles. Handing out a bag of popcorn is an opportunity for personal contact. Print your theme on the bag. As advertising manager for a consulting organization, I called the *Harvard Business Review* and asked what was the most disruptive and intrusive advertisement they had run. The response was they hadn't run it yet, but suggested enclosing our brochure in the shrink wrap on the outside of editions mailed to subscribers. We did. More than 200,000 subscribers saw our brochure on top of the magazine when removing the clear plastic wrap. We were overwhelmed with responses.

Seventh Principle
Maneuver

The main thing for an army is calm elasticity.
If it has this, the men's strength will be sufficient.

— "Wu Chi on *The Art of War*"
Fourth Century B.C.

> ### STRATEGICALLY
> Maneuver is a way of thinking about how you move
> to a position of competitive advantage.
>
> ### TACTICALLY
> Maneuver allows you to concentrate or disperse.

The easiest routes are often the most heavily defended; the longest way round can be the shortest way home.

 Maneuver is simply a process of moving and acting in a way that puts your competitor at a disadvantage. Without thinking about how you can maneuver, the idea of fighting when you are outnumbered is ludicrous. When thinking about maneuvering, you understand how to attack specific segments, markets, or accounts where you can win.

Maneuver is the dynamic element of marketing. It's the means that enables small companies to compete against large ones and large ones to get bigger.

Maneuvers around enemy lines to weak points are as old as warfare. The essence of both military and marketing maneuvers is that the way to avoid what is strong is to attack what is weak. Successful marketing managers are always looking for unoccupied or lightly defended positions in the market. Examples of maneuvering around competitive strength can be found in every industry.

In the auto industry, the original Ford Mustang was introduced as a sports roadster that did not compete with the family sedans of the time. The success of this approach was revealed in surveys indicating that single females were the most frequent owners. Chrysler earned a new position in the market by introducing the minivan as a viable alternative to family sedans and station wagons. The minivan bred the sport utility vehicle, another distinct product category in which early entrants had limited competition.

In the computer industry, Dell achieved rapid growth by maneuvering around the existing reseller structure and heading directly to the end customer. This approach won strong support and volume sales from purchasing agents in industry and government.

The initial success of many Japanese products in the American market has been the result of an end run around existing products with entries at lower price points and features. The combination works.

LEVERAGE OPPORTUNITIES

Maneuvers aimed at gaining leverage from the buying and selling relationship must be designed to give benefits to both parties. Mutual leverage is the key to customer loyalty programs: The seller benefits from a revenue stream, and the buyer benefits from the reward program.

If the marketer gives the customer too little leverage, the sale may be lost, along with the opportunity for a long-term relationship. If the marketer gives the customer too much leverage, the sale and the continuing relationship will be unprofitable.

Buyer and seller relationships work best when there is balanced leverage. The seller must give benefits to the buyer; more benefits yield more leverage. The buyer must be a profitable factor in the marketing relationship—the more profitable the sale, the more anxious the seller is to give continued service.

Retailers who specialize in a limited number of brands are attempting to leverage their relationship with their suppliers while they concentrate on a segment of the market. Another kind of leverage is used by retailers who sell a wide variety of brands; they leverage their relationship with suppliers to get the best deal. Both types of leverage work.

A retailer relates, "We visit our key manufacturers every 6 months at their headquarters. Our managers have prepared presentations concerning what we need, and the manufacturer listens—I mean he really listens." What a difference from the normal seller and buyer meetings, where only the seller makes the presentation.

The rule of leveraging is that you must give leverage to get leverage. The business that gives no leverage gets none in return.

TACTICS FOR MANEUVERING

Engage in a frontal attack only when you have overwhelming strength and can generate momentum. Sheer numbers of resources and advertising power may not be enough to dislodge a competitor who is occupying a strong position. When a business guerrilla launches a frontal attack, it's called a waste of money.

Flanking by going around strength works. We see it every day in retailing. Von Clausewitz says, "Flank and rear attacks are by far the most successful."

The objective of the marketing blitz is to achieve a maximum number of contacts in a minimum amount of time. It is an attempt to break through by attacking over a wide front, bypassing all resistance. What is important is penetration, not overwhelming those who are resisting.

There is a military maxim that the greatest cause of defeat is victory. The more successful we get, the greater the tendency to stop doing those things that made us successful. That's when marketing relationships deteriorate and customers go elsewhere.

Choose the Best Maneuvers

*Both advantage and danger
are inherent in maneuvering
for an advantageous position.*

One who is not acquainted with the designs of his neighbors should not enter into alliances with them. Those who do not know the conditions of mountains and forests, hazardous defiles, marshes and swamps, cannot conduct the march of an army. Those who do not use local guides are unable to obtain the advantages of the ground.

—Sun Tzu

A LESSON FROM GIDEON

The Bible tells the story of the battle of the Midianites near Mt. Gilboa. Gideon, during his personal reconnaissance of the enemy, noticed that the enemy sentries were nervous.

To create panic in the enemy lines, Gideon planned a night attack with a relatively small force. Each of his 300 men was issued a trumpet, a pitcher, and a torch. Convinced that the Lord was on his side, he gave the battle order—"the sword of the Lord and of Gideon." The men lit the torches, hid them in the pitchers, slung their trumpets, grasped their swords, and quietly went to predetermined positions.

When the Midianites changed their watch at midnight, Gideon gave his signal. His men blew their trumpets and waved their torches. In the resulting panic in the Midianite camp, tribe fought tribe while Gideon and his Israelites stood and watched. And thus another battle was won by the strategy of an observant commander who understood how to use deception to confuse the opponent.

The principles that Gideon used make sense for every marketing commander:

1. Personal reconnaissance gives a feel for the right maneuver.
2. Attention to detail and sound staff work help.
3. Keep it simple.

THE RIGHT MANEUVER VARIES WITH THE CIRCUMSTANCES

Frontal attack: A head-on attack, where the biggest force wins. The frontal attack is a direct assault on a competitor. While most marketing managers and guerrilla entrepreneurs should avoid head-on attacks, this rule has exceptions. For example, a head-on attack into a fast-growing market might not really be a head-on attack.

Flanking attack: An end run to an unoccupied or lightly defended position. The flanking attack is the most frequently used of all maneuvers. Unlike the frontal attack, in a flanking attack the strength is concentrated against weakness. Flanking attacks are entries into new markets, and this can be the most profitable way to grow.

Attack in echelon: Concentration of your strengths. Gain entry with a strong or unique product, and build brand strength from this relationship.

Relocate the Battle: Finding a new war. Every new shopping mall is an attempt to relocate the battle geographically. When an advertising agency executive found his client thinking about a new agency, he launched into a discussion on what the client needed to do in order to succeed. He said, "I didn't even talk about the competitor. I merely changed the battlefield."

Blitz: Bypassing strong points. Whether in personal contacts, direct mail, or advertising, the marketing blitz is a short-term mass attack.

Encirclement: Denying key resources. Expand into all the locations your competitor would like to own.

Defense: Maintaining position. The marketing defense should most often be a strategic interval—time to prepare another offense.

Fabian: Refusing battle. The marketing application is to not engage in competitive advertising and to use the funds for another activity.

Guerrilla: Taking what you can get. Be mobile, flexible, and superior at the critical point of attack.

General Pogo's strategy: You have met the enemy. Attack yourself.

Retreat: Getting out of the business.

Flanking Often Wins

What is difficult about maneuvering
for favorable positions beforehand is
to make the devious route the most direct
and to turn disadvantage to advantage.

By forcing the enemy to deviate and slow down his march by luring him
with a bait, you may set out after he does and arrive at the battlefield before
him. One able to do this shows the knowledge of artifice of deviation.

—Sun Tzu

THE INDIRECT APPROACH

The indirect approach is a devious version of flanking. The differences are subtle, and aimed at keeping your opponent from knowing that you are aiming your strength against a weakness.

Do not ever go head-on into strength. Of roughly 300 campaigns covered in one military text, in only 6 was a decisive result obtained by a direct approach to the main army of the enemy. Remember Pickett's failed charge at Gettysburg. When the British tried an uphill bayonet charge at Breed's Hill (Bunker Hill), they lost 1000 of 2500 troops.

FLANKING CAN BE A SHORT ROUTE TO SUCCESS

The marketing maneuver is often a flanking maneuver that locates the battle in a place where you can have superiority. "To be where your customers are and your competitor isn't" is the easiest way to marketing victory. In business as in war, the best approach is one that gives you the greatest superiority at the decisive point.

Products have life cycles; so do distribution strategies. For years the only copy machines were made by Xerox. Xeroxing became a descriptive term for getting a copy made. Xerox dominated the market. Then a tiny company that was barely making it by selling copiers through its own offices moved into an overlooked distribution channel: the office products dealer. As copiers became simple and cheap, the old distribution system became a dinosaur.

There is a difference between doing the unconventional and ignoring the principles of marketing. When Chick-fil-A tried to move into a shopping mall, the owners of the mall tried to discourage him. Says founder Truitt Cathy, "The thinking at the time was that a fast-food restaurant had no place in a shopping mall." The indirect approach to a new position caught on, and today Chick-fil-A often shares the mall food court with other fast-food restaurants.

In the auto wars, the Germans did not attack the larger American cars head on; instead, they maneuvered to the lightly defended flank at the low end of the market with the tiny Volkswagen. The Japanese copied the tactic with the Toyota and the Honda and the. . . .

Holiday Inn innovated in the lodging business by locating motels at the edge of town, where they did not compete with the downtown hotels. Dell maneuvered to a direct-to-customer distribution channel where it bypassed the retailer and controlled its message. The rest is history. There are thousands of variations of the marketing maneuver to a lightly defended position.

The flanking attack can establish a base for invading the core market—or it can become the core. When Michelin innovated steel-belted radials, it eventually shifted the tire market from bias-ply to radial.

Concentrate
or Divide

Move when it is advantageous
and change tactics by dispersal
and concentration of your troops.

Now, war is based on deception. When campaigning, be swift as the wind; in leisurely march, be majestic as the forest; in raiding and plundering, be fierce as fire; in standing, be firm as the mountains. When hiding, be as unfathomable as things behind the clouds; when moving, fall like a thunderclap. When you plunder the countryside, divide your forces. When you conquer territory, defend strategic points.

Weigh the situation before you move. He who knows the artifice of deviation will be victorious. Such is the art of maneuvering.

—Sun Tzu

THINK BIG;
WORK SMALL

Think big about what you want to achieve. Think small about how to achieve it. Concentrate on the individuals and small groups and their motivation. The macro models are merely a collage of those teams.

"Almost everyone is for decentralization—from themselves up, but not from themselves down."

—General W. L. Creech
The Five Pillars of TQM

CENTRALIZE OR DECENTRALIZE

Segmenting the market is a way to win. The battle cry for segmentation is "target, target, target." Pick a niche, or a particle of the market, and serve that segment better than anyone else.

The first rule of segmentation is that you must offer the customer a clearly differentiated product that fills (or creates) a need.

The cycle of segmentation is a series of changes in our view of marketing concentration:

- First comes the product focus. The needs of the customer are overshadowed by an emphasis on how we design and manufacture the product.
- Next follows a market focus. The question of how we are going to improve distribution turns our thinking to how to reach specific segments of the market.
- Finally, the customer focus emerges. The organization sees the customer as an individual with whom a relationship must be established.

Smaller companies that concentrate on a very specific segment of the market are the most expert at getting close to the customer. They succeed by concentrating on doing what they know and knowing what they do. You see this type of segmentation in children's bookstores, paint stores, and ethnic restaurants and food stores.

In niche marketing, all resources are concentrated on a single product category in a tightly focused marketing opportunity. The tighter the niche, the more sure you are of "owning" the segment. Although the narrowness of the segment would appear to make you more vulnerable, this is not the case. A walk past the specialty stores in any shopping mall, or a visit to a yogurt stand, can prove the viability of segmentation.

Honda calls its segmentation strategy "localization." The company builds facilities where the markets are, earns profits, and reinvests them on the spot—that brings it close to the customer.

Market from Strength

A wise general in his deliberations
must consider both favorable
and unfavorable factors.

By taking into account the favorable factors, he makes his plan feasible; by taking into account the unfavorable, he may avoid possible disasters.

There are some roads which must not be followed, some troops which must not be attacked, some cities which must not be assaulted, some ground which must not be contested, and some commands of the sovereign which must not be obeyed.

Hence, the general who thoroughly understands the advantages that accompany variation of tactics knows how to employ troops.

The general who does not is unable to use the terrain to his advantage even though he is well acquainted with it.

—Sun Tzu

GAINING LEVERAGE

Critical to leveraging is the existence of a working relationship between buyer and seller. This can be at one of three levels: consumer (mass), customer (a person or entity that buys things), or client (more personal). When a customer becomes a client, you have more leverage.

133

REINFORCE STRENGTH; MINIMIZE WEAKNESS

Attila the Hun concentrated on terror, Frederick the Great was a master of maneuver, and Joan of Arc built her army on charismatic leadership. It's all part of doing well what you do well.

Focus your offensive by allocating the most resources to whomever or whatever is getting results. Maximize support where it generates the most business. Your best customers are your best prospects. Your best product lines are your best vehicles for more business. McDonald's business was better when it concentrated on promoting to kids (its best customers) and worse when it shifted its attention to adults.

Concentrate your time and efforts on providing the resources to continue the successful advance, and don't spend time and resources shoring up weak products and weak attacks. Reinforcing weakness leverages weakness. Reinforcing strength leverages strength. There's no question which is better.

It's not the management system that governs the choice between reinforcing strength or weakness; rather, the choice of the attack system dictates the management system. A system of reinforcing weakness requires centralized authority radiating from headquarters. A system of reinforcing strength thrives in a decentralized culture.

The franchise system reinforces strength. The brand name, identity, products, and services are common to all locations. The management and personnel are local. Many organizations will decentralize the "front room," where personal service is critical, and centralize the "back-room" functions, where technological strengths can be utilized.

Marketing from strength works in every organization and every product line. You see it when companies prune product lines to concentrate on their core business. You see it in advertising when companies focus on promoting premier brands and products. The strength of the discounter is price and selection. The strength of the department store and clothing specialist is style and brand names. The strength of the boutique is special-ization. All succeed when they reinforce strength.

Eighth Principle
Concentration of Resources

The five weapons have five uses.

The long defend the short and the short assist the long.

If you fight with them in turn it makes for delay.

But if with all together it makes for strength.

Regard the position carefully and act together.

This is called mutual action.

—"The Precepts of Ssu Ma Jang Chu"
Fourth Century B.C.

STRATEGICALLY
The concentration is a management commitment
to a marketing offensive.

TACTICALLY
The concentration is always of strength
against weakness.

Mass sufficiently superior force at the decisive place and time.

The fundamental strategy for success in the marketing attack is to plan a concentration of resources where

1. Needs have been identified.
2. Competition is weak.
3. Profit potential is high.

The highest levels of success occur when resources are focused where decisive results can be achieved profitably.

Attacks succeed because a wise strategist concentrates the available forces. A bold move aimed with surgical precision at a weak point can bring victory at little cost. Eisenhower did this with the combined forces on D-Day. MacArthur's island-hopping campaign in the Pacific was a series of mass invasions. Schwarzkopf liberated Kuwait with forces concentrated at weak points.

Frederick the Great referred to concentration as the "main · effort." He said, "If you want to fight a battle, you must draw together as many troops as you can, you cannot use them better anywhere else. Little minds try to defend everything at once, but sensible people look at the main point only; they parry the worst blows and stand a little hurt if thereby they avoid a greater one. If you try to hold everything, you hold nothing."

The essence of concentration of resources is *the concentration of your strength against the opponent's weakness.* Marketing concentration is not a mere mass of numbers, but rather a focusing of your marketing strategy and tactics.

When thinking about where you are going to concentrate, look for the weakness of the opponent's strength. This is most often found at a junction. It could be between geographic locations, between product lines, at the extreme low end or high end, or wherever there is a dividing line.

If your marketing force is weaker than your competitor's, *and* if you fight head to head against your competitor, then you'll end up with a very bad headache—or no head at all.

Napoleon wrote, "It should be adopted as a principle never to allow intervals through which the enemy can penetrate between the different corps forming the line of battle."

Concentration requires a decision to allocate resources. The question is always, do you commit your full resources to a specific effort (bet the company), or do you hold something in reserve—and if so, how much?

How much to concentrate is a quandary for us in everything we do, from allocation of time through planning financial expenditures. Two simple rules govern concentration of resources:

1. It is an error to attempt to concentrate everywhere; the result is no concentration.
2. The more tightly focused your concentration, the more sure you are to have winning superiority.

CONCENTRATION OF ADVERTISING

Advertising is a marketing weapon that demonstrates its firepower in capturing share of mind. Advertising is not a strategy; it is simply a weapon in your arsenal. A small advertising expenditure is often no more effective than no expenditure. You must find a way to be heard above the noise of all the other ads that are competing for attention. What you do in advertising and promotion must be unique and so carefully targeted that it pierces the clutter and reaches the objective. If you cannot achieve the critical marketing mass, you might be better off spending your money elsewhere. Some successful companies concentrate on advertising, and others do little or no advertising.

In war, the tank serves as an offensive force that solves all its tactical problems by attacking. We can go broke trying a similar tactic with advertising. The first rule of advertising is to target the message and media to the market.

A question often asked is, "Can smart dimes beat dumb dollars?" That is, can creativity beat mass? Mundane volume can overwhelm the market, but even the most creative ads need exposure in order to be effective.

Consistency is a form of concentration. Repetition builds identity. Coca-Cola did it with a bottle, Maytag's consistency is the lonely repairman, Marlboro has the Marlboro man, and Disney's consistent image is a mouse named Mickey.

As surely as consistency works in advertising, so does inconsistency breed failure. Too many changes in the advertising message confuses the brand identity.

Good advertising requires good strategy focused on selling the product. When the strategy is weak, the execution often shifts from selling the product to selling the lifestyle. The message about buying the brand gets lost.

140

When the execution is weak, the message doesn't penetrate. When the execution overpowers the message, the customer remembers the execution and forgets the brand name.

CONCENTRATE ON CONCENTRATING

Other methods of concentration are discussed in the following pages.

Not all of the ways to target customer segments have been tried or discovered. The winners will be those who find new ways to "own" a segment, continue with that strategy as long as it works, and adapt new strategies when the old one becomes outmoded.

You can concentrate on your strengths by leveraging off the things you do well. You can concentrate on attacking yourself in quality, costs, or performance. You can even concentrate on simplicity—because, after all, a simple message is simply a concentration of words.

Concentrate Strength against Weakness

*The law of successful operations is to avoid
the enemy's strength and strike his weakness.*

*Now, the laws of military operations are like water. The tendency of
water is to flow from heights to lowlands. Water changes its course in
accordance with the contours of the land. The soldier works out his victory in accordance with the situation of the enemy.*

> *Consequently, the art of using troops is this:*
> *When ten to the enemy's one, surround him.*
> *When five times his strength, attack him.*
> *If double his strength, engage him.*
> *If equally matched, be capable of dividing him.*
> *If less in number, be capable of defending yourself.*
> *And if in all respects unfavorable, be capable of eluding him.*

> *Hence, a weak force will eventually fall captive to a strong one if it
simply holds ground and conducts a desperate defense.*
> *Now, the key to military operations lies in cautiously studying the
enemy's designs. Concentrate your forces in the main direction against the
enemy and from a distance of a thousand li you can kill his general. This is
called the ability to achieve one's aim in an artful and ingenious manner.*

—Sun Tzu

"The best strategy is to be very strong, first generally; then at the decisive point . . . there is no more imperative and no simpler law for strategy than to keep the forces concentrated."

—Carl von Clausewitz
On War

FIND AN OVERWHELMING SUPERIORITY

The math of business is as simple as the ratios for competing that Sun Tzu set forth in 500 B.C.: Never give a competitor an equal chance.

The Red Chinese believed that victory can be achieved only by striking in selected areas where overwhelming superiority can be achieved. They considered a superiority of 3 to 1 to be the minimum, but much higher ratios—up to 10 to 1—were preferred.

Attack vigorously when you can concentrate a superiority against a weak spot in the competitor's line.

The marketing attack demands that you have superiority. History has proven that when significantly superior forces are concentrated on the main effort, victory is assured. The question always is: How many resources can we allocate profitably? The risk is always that when allocating too few, you lose. Concentration works in everything and everywhere:

- *Strategy:* Apply consistent pressure on achieving key strategic initiatives.
- *Advertising:* Use repetition of a clear, distinctive benefit.
- *Sales promotion:* Reinforce the advertising message.
- *Selling:* Focus on your unique selling proposition.
- *Leadership:* Concentrate on developing people.
- *Management:* Be consistently predictable.

Sometimes the concentration is simply intensity of effort on a single task.

The blitz is a type of marketing concentration in which you concentrate your efforts on a single neighborhood, market segment, or type of customer for a limited period of time.

Attain Relative Superiority at the Decisive Point

If we are able to use many to strike few at the selected place, those we deal with will be in dire straits.

Accordingly, by exposing the enemy's dispositions and remaining invisible ourselves, we can keep our forces concentrated, while the enemy's must be divided. We can form a single united body at one place, while the enemy must scatter his forces at ten places.

The spot where we intend to fight must not be made known. In this way, the enemy must take precautions at many places against the attack. The more places he must guard, the fewer his troops we shall have to face at any given point.

For if he prepares to the front his rear will be weak; and if to the rear, his front will be fragile. If he strengthens his left, his right will be vulnerable; and if his right gets strengthened, there will be few troops on his left. If he sends reinforcements everywhere, he will be weak everywhere.

Numerical weakness comes from having to prepare against possible attacks; numerical strength from compelling the enemy to make these preparations against us.

—Sun Tzu

THE ESSENCE OF GREAT STRATEGY IS TO CONCENTRATE SUPERIOR STRENGTH AT THE WEAKEST POINT

In his book *On War*, von Clausewitz says,

144

"Where absolute superiority is not attainable, you must produce a relative superiority at the decisive point by making skillful use of what you have."

Nowhere in marketing is the lesson for victory so clearly stated in a single sentence:

Use available resources to produce
a relative superiority and deliver that superiority
to a decisive point.

Small units win when they achieve relative superiority. This is the principle used by guerrilla warriors and niche marketers. Achieving relative superiority has been a fundamental strategy of every winning general.

The marketing application is that you should not attack the other company, but rather concentrate local superiority on specific competitive products, services, locations, or distribution channels.

The essence of relative superiority is to deliver maximum power at a weak point where it makes a difference. Relative superiority is often achieved through a combination of secrecy and surprise.

To achieve relative superiority, think in terms of running small, consistent ads in the same place in the same publications, finding an unoccupied niche, or dramatically demonstrating a unique superiority. An inferior force can think strategically about winning if it can achieve relative superiority at points of contact, such as training, credit, warranty, technology, sales ability, or service. This is the way small companies get to be big companies.

Achieve the Critical Marketing Mass

---

*It is ten to one
when we attack him at one place,
which means we are numerically superior.*

One who sets the entire army in motion with impedimenta to pursue an advantageous position, will be slow to attain it. If he abandons the camp and all the impedimenta to contend for advantage, the baggage and stores will be lost.

It follows that when the army rolls up the armour and sets out speedily, stopping neither day nor night and marching at double speed for a hundred li to wrest an advantage, the commander of three divisions will be captured. The vigorous troops will arrive first and the feeble will straggle along behind, so that if this method is used, only one-tenth of the army will arrive. In a forced march of fifty li the commander of the first and van division will fall, and using this method but half of the army will arrive. In a forced march of thirty li, but two-thirds will arrive. Hence, the army will be lost without baggage train; and it cannot survive without provisions, nor can it last long without sources of supplies.

—Sun Tzu

CONCENTRATE ENERGY TO OVERCOME THE NATURAL BUYING INERTIA

Napoleon said quite simply, "Force must be concentrated at one point and as soon as the breach is made, the equilibrium is broken."

Attaining the critical marketing mass is the way to achieve victory. You need to search for a critical point in the marketplace where you can have an advantage. Then you deploy your resources so that you control these critical factors. You gain market share where you have an advantage—if you have a big enough advantage, you should be able to get 100 percent of the market.

The speed of the Mongols invariably gave them a superiority of force at the decisive point—the ultimate aim of all tactics. By seizing the initiative and exploiting their mobility, the Mongol commanders, rather than their foes, selected the point of decision.

Weight multiplied by velocity achieves breakthroughs and builds momentum, in marketing as in nuclear fission.

The ultimate judge of whether you have obtained the critical mass is the customer. His or her decision to buy is the critical vote.

Jo-Ann Fabrics has few competitors in its core fabric business. It does something that few others do, and that even fewer do well. It is in a business that is subject to the whims of fashion, and it has achieved critical mass by

- Stocking a wide selection of fabrics
- Cutting every order to the customer's specifications

It takes a great deal of insight to determine the critical issues because the fog of business masks what is really happening. Of all the things that need to be done, many are good business, some are important, but only a few are really critical.

The critical marketing issue may be the right product concept, the right marketing channel, or attacking the right market, or it may be elements that extend across the entire process, from material sourcing to distribution. In every aspect of business, there is a critical mass to be achieved. Go for it.

Build Winning Teamwork

*They will come to each other's assistance
just as the left hand helps the right.*

Strike at the head of the snake Shuai Ran, and you will be attacked by its tail. Strike at its tail, and you will be attacked by its head. Strike at its middle, and you will be attacked by both its head and its tail.

Should one ask: "Can troops be made capable of such instantaneous coordination as the Shuai Ran?" I reply: "They can." For the men of Wu and the men of Yue are enemies, yet if they are crossing a river in the same boat and are caught by a storm, they will come to each other's assistance just as the left hand helps the right.

Hence, it is not sufficient to rely upon tethering of the horses and the burying of the chariots. The principle of military administration is to achieve a uniform level of courage.

Thus, a skillful general conducts his army just as if he were leading a single man, willy-nilly, by the hand.

The general principles applicable to an invading force are that the deeper you penetrate into hostile territory, the greater will be the solidarity of your troops, and thus the defenders cannot overcome you.

—Sun Tzu

"Four brave men who do not know each other well, will not dare attack a lion. Four less brave who know each other well, sure of reliability, and consequently of mutual aid, will attack resolutely. There is the science of organization of armies in a nutshell."

—Ardant du Picq
Battle Studies

EIGHTH PRINCIPLE

TEAMWORK WINS

Evidence of the importance of teamwork between the strategist and the tactician can be seen in the development of the Israeli Merkava tank. No nation so small had ever built a tank.

The eight-person design crew (a good team size) included engineers, model builders, and tank warfare veterans (a good mix of experts). Team leader Tai followed the philosophy that good design is not the result of inspiration, but rather of slow, often painfully slow, problem-solving processes (as it is in business).

The design was radical compared to that of other armies' tanks. The engine was placed forward as a buffer—this allowed for innovative rear doors for crew escape or for picking up wounded. Because diesel fuel does not ignite easily, fuel reservoirs were also up front for further protection. Small-caliber ammunition that is not prone to explode when hit formed a buffer inside the hull. Cannon shells that do explode easily were stored down low in protective containers.

The Merkava has proved itself in battle: Wounded soldiers have been rescued, and burn cases have been rare. The Merkava is one of the least expensive tanks of its class. Says one armor specialist at the Pentagon, "This tank is overweight, undergunned, and too slow. Even so, it is one of the world's best tanks."

The design process never stops. Every engineer assigned to the project has been sent into battle to analyze the tank's performance firsthand. New versions are continually being developed.

The marketing parallel is simply that the best products come from teamwork between those who know the technology and those who are experienced in the field. Neither sales nor marketing has any monopoly on information. Planning is important;

you've got to have the right strategy. The implementation, and doing it right, is also critical.

The chief executive of Nestlé says the business lesson he learned from mountaineering is: "You learn early on that you're better off working in a team. It's how you'll survive. There's nothing worse than having a weak team."

Teamwork reduces costly errors and increases the possibility of brilliant solutions. A team of experienced people who coordinate their efforts and are concentrated on an objective consistently outperforms individuals who are trying to achieve the same goals.

One-person efforts are out. Teamwork is in—if you want to win.

Ninth Principle
Economy of Force

*Strike at the immobility of weakness
and avoid that of strength.*

*If you use a small force it must be strong,
and if you employ a large one it must be disciplined*

*In using a large force,
it should be able to advance and hold its ground.*

*In using a small force,
it should be able to advance and retire.*

"The Precepts of Ssu Ma Jang Chu"
Fourth Century B.C.

┌───┐
│   │
│   *STRATEGICALLY*   │
│   Economy of force requires a return on investment. │
│   │
│   *TACTICALLY*   │
│ Economy of force allocates all resources to the main effort. │
│   │
└───┘

Assess accurately where you employ your resources.

 This military principle reveals the other side of the coin from concentration of resources. When you concentrate in one area, you will be weak in other areas. Once you have decided where to concentrate, economy of force deals with the allocation of resources.

The word *economy* in "economy of force" does not refer to economizing; rather, it refers to the effective use of resources. Marshal Foch described economy of force as the "art of pouring out all of one's resources on a given spot, of making use there of all of one's troops."

Economy of force has two dimensions:

1. *Efficiency*—avoiding the waste of time and resources
2. *Effectiveness*—getting the right results

An orientation toward efficiency makes us get every person and screw in place in order to maximize the more quantifiable (and countable) activities of corporate firepower. This leads to numbers-oriented activities such as counting the resources that will be expended.

An orientation toward effectiveness makes us provide the systems and structures that develop the qualitative (and less measurable) aspects of corporate firepower. This leads to results-oriented thinking, such as how resources can be allocated to achieve the objective.

If we are not effective, we have no need to be efficient. Ask Texas Instruments about its failed home computer effort, Ford about its Edsel, or the corner grocer who went out of business.

We need to be efficient, but not at the expense of delivering sufficient fighting power at the point of sale. An inefficient victory is bad, but not as bad as losing—which is extremely inefficient.

The key to success is to align corporate resources to focus on predetermined strategic initiatives.

DO NOT WASTE ENERGY

Forces are wasted in actions like the Battle of Leyte Gulf, where Admiral Halsey took his great Third Fleet on a high-speed dash of 300 miles against a decoy, then turned to pursue the main force, which he never reached. Similarly, d'Erlon's reserve in the Waterloo campaign marched and countermarched between two French armies, aiding neither and unable to influence either battle.

This chopping and changing is analogous to the entrepreneur who opens branch operations in distant cities and spends so much time traveling back and forth that he can barely find time to run the business.

HANDLING INTERNAL CONFLICTS

It is in the search for efficiencies at headquarters and in the profit analysis of campaigns that marketing managers will have their greatest problems with the bureaucracy.

1. Finance and administrative officers are more easily positioned to attack plans and performance, while sales and marketing management must defend them. The continu-

ous defense is untenable because you must always defend at the position of the attacker's choice. The problem is exacerbated by the nature of headquarters conferences:

- The attackers often have little knowledge of the reality of the field situation. Since they have not been in contact with customers, they do not ask the right questions.
- Marketing is often in a position where it can only defend its plans and performance because the attackers have neither plans nor performance.

2. Since finance and administration do not become identified with product failures or failure to achieve quotas, they escape the negative ratings when things don't work. It is generally true that those who can be rated on specifics tend to be underrated.

Build Internal Strength

The general who advances
without coveting fame
and retreats without fearing disgrace,
whose only purpose is to protect his people
and promote the best interests of his sovereign,
is the precious jewel of the state.

If fighting does not stand a good chance of victory, you need not to fight even though the sovereign has issued an order to engage.

Hence, if, in the light of the prevailing situation, fighting is sure to result in victory, then you may decide to fight even though the sovereign has issued an order not to engage.

—Sun Tzu

"In military affairs there are four opportunities.

1. *Spirit. This is when the men are influenced in their feelings entirely by one man.*
2. *Geography. This is when the path is narrow and the way is steep and so makes a great stronghold where ten men can hold a thousand at bay.*
3. *Circumstances. This is when by good management in using spies and sending light troops the enemy's forces are scattered and their loyalty to their superiors undermined.*
4. *Power. This is when naves and linch-pins of the chariots are tight, and oars and rudders of the ships well fitted, the officers well trained for battle and horses broken to the right pace."*

—"Wu Chi on *The Art of War*"
Fourth Century B.C.

155

THE
JEWEL OF
THE STATE

In 1943, General Robert Wood Johnson established a 300-word credo for Johnson & Johnson. The one-page document focused on service to four audiences. The first paragraph was devoted primarily to customers and reads as follows:

"We believe our first responsibility is to the doctors, nurses, and patients, to mothers and fathers and all others who use our product and services.

In meeting their needs everything we do must be of high quality. We must constantly strive to reduce our costs in order to maintain reasonable prices. Customers' orders must be serviced promptly and accurately. Our suppliers and distributors must have an opportunity to make a fair profit."

The paragraphs that follow presented the credo as it related to employees, communities, and stockholders. This credo gave the company the internal strength to go from a small, privately held enterprise to a worldwide corporation that is recognized for its integrity. The credo can be read in many languages on the company's Web site and on office walls.

B. H. Liddell Hart comments in *Strategy* that "the downfall of civilized states tends to come not from the direct assaults of foes but from internal decays combined with the consequences of exhaustion in war." Like Napoleon in his march on Moscow, some companies are destroyed as much by their own exertions as by the enemy.

Too many business battles end because the company runs out of financial resources. Your cash flow and profit projections must plan for contingencies.

Recently, we received an email a restaurant owner sent to all his customers complaining that local customers were not supporting his establishment. A few weeks later he closed the restaurant. Somehow he failed to understand that it was not the customers' fault that he was going out of business.

Almost every successful penetration of a new business into a new industry has succeeded because the new business offered more features and benefits at a price that represented a distinctly better value. Venture into the market with a "me too" product and you'll soon be venturing home with your entire inventory.

Many old brand names are gone. For example, a kitchen cleanser named Bon Ami had a market share of 85 percent. Today it is difficult to find on the shelf. Evidence shows that Bon Ami suffered this decline as a result of competitive pressures *and* mismanagement.

In trying to rescue failing organizations, there is a point beyond which persistence of effort becomes folly. This problem is often seen in companies on the verge of bankruptcy as management ignores every good business practice in an effort to survive.

Choose
Your Battles

If not in the interests of the state,
do not act.
If you are not sure of success,
do not use troops.
If you are not in danger,
do not fight a battle.

A sovereign should not launch a war simply out of anger, nor should a general fight a war simply out of resentment. Take action if it is to your advantage; cancel the action if it is not. An angered man can be happy again, just as a resentful one can feel pleased again, but a state that has perished can never revive, nor can a dead man be brought back to life.

Therefore, with regard to the matter of war, the enlightened ruler is prudent, and the good general is full of caution. Thus, the state is kept secure and the army preserved.

—Sun Tzu

One who gains one victory becomes Emperor;
One who gains two, a King;
One who gains three, Lord Protector;
One who gains four is exhausted;
One who gains five victories suffers a calamity.
So those who have gained an Empire by many victories are few,
but those who have lost one in this way are many.

—"Wu Chi on *The Art of War*"
Fourth Century B.C.

DO NOT FIGHT BATTLES
YOU CANNOT WIN—OR WIN THOSE
THAT LOSE THE WAR

All managers are politicians in the sense they have developed the ability to deal with people. Too little or too much "politics" can be disastrous. Your internal political position is determined by what you do and what you do not do.

The province of the marketing manager is to provide product leadership. The province of the sales manager is to provide distribution leadership. Neither can do the job of the other. These restrictions are not caused by personal failings, but rather by positions on the team.

Marketing and selling must be mutually supportive forces in the business battle. Every business function must be focused on serving the customer. Too often, departments play adversarial roles. These civil wars only dissipate resources. Success comes when managers representing all corporate disciplines stand tall as they congratulate one another on their respective strengths.

Heed the sound advice from Wu Chi when he warns about gaining too many victories. This advice applies to corporations that grow too fast and to the battles of corporate politics.

You can meet disaster when you fight too many battles in the internal struggles of corporate politics. Fight the ones that really count and don't get caught in small turf wars. We see the consequences of fighting too many battles when organizations fill positions from outside because capable people inside have made too many enemies by winning too often.

As bosses change and companies merge, you will have a wide array of superiors. Some will challenge your survival ability. Although you may need to be in a survival mode to live through these psychotic executives, beware of the tendency to remain in the survival mode after these executives leave.

Set your pace so you can consolidate your gains and organize your defenses—so that you have a solid base for organizing the next initiative.

Be Efficient

Those adept in employing troops do not require a second levy of conscripts or more than two provisionings.

They carry military supplies from the homeland and make up for their provisions relying on the enemy. Thus the army will be always plentifully provided.

When a country is impoverished by military operations, it is because an army far from its homeland needs a distant transportation. Being forced to carry supplies for great distances renders the people destitute. On the other hand, the local price of commodities normally rises high in the area near the military camps. The rising prices cause financial resources to be drained away.

When the resources are exhausted, the peasantry will be afflicted with urgent exactions. With this depletion of strength and exhaustion of wealth, every household in the homeland is left empty.

Seven-tenths of the people's income is dissipated and six-tenths of the government's revenue is paid for broken-down chariots, worn-out horses, armour and helmets, arrows and crossbows, halberds and bucklers, spears and body shields, draught oxen and heavy wagons.

Hence, a wise general is sure of getting provisions from the enemy countries.

—Sun Tzu

PROFIT IS A REQUIREMENT FOR SURVIVAL

Economy of force requires that you make a profit analysis of every campaign. Your expenditures to achieve victory must yield profitable results.

Field Marshal Montgomery's Operation Market Garden in World War II was described by a military historian as "a fifty-mile salient leading nowhere." A movie on the advance was titled *A Bridge Too Far*.

"A bridge too far" can happen when organizations expand too rapidly. The infamous dot-com collapse in the computer industry was a major example.

We see other disastrous effects of violating the principle of economy of force when companies go on an acquisition binge, or when retailers open too many branches too rapidly, or when franchisors overfranchise. The problem is not the forward movement, but rather the too-rapid rate of the forward movement. Like an overly fertilized plant, the organization is exhausted by its own growth. The financial structure, management systems, and human resources need time to mature.

It is possible for a rapidly growing business in a rapidly growing industry to fail because it expands beyond its cash-flow capabilities. As in war, when the advance gets ahead of the supply lines, the unit is highly vulnerable. In any rapidly growing business, the first economic slowdown can be a catastrophe.

When I called on small-business owners who were in trouble, I could tell where the owner had begun her or his career by watching where she or he spent time. Someone who started out in service would be in the service department trying to service his or her way out of the problem. An owner with a financial background would be in the office trying to administrate his way out of the problem. In times of business stress, we revert to our basic expertise to solve problems. We do what we know, and too often that is not what needs to be done.

Tenth Principle
Command Structure

*In war, it is not handling an army that is difficult,
but getting men to handle it.*

*It is not getting them to handle it that is difficult,
but getting them to handle it properly.*

*It is not knowing how to do it that is difficult,
but being able to carry it out.*

"The Precepts of Ssu Ma Jang Chu"
Fourth Century B.C.

┌───┐
│   │
│   *STRATEGICALLY*   │
│   Command structure provides the links in the chain │
│   so that all the other principles can be effective. │
│   │
│   *TACTICALLY*   │
│   Command structure provides for both the unleashing │
│   and the coalescence of human resources.   │
│   │
└───┘

The management process unleashes the power of human resources.

 The U.S. Army calls this principle "unity of command." The point is that there must be coordination of action toward a common goal, and that this coordination is best achieved by vesting a single commander with authority.

Napoleon considered unity of command to be the first prerequisite for a successful war. To him, this meant the marshaling of forces under his direction. It is to be expected that strong commanders should consider strong unified control to be an organizational requirement. However, just as unity of command was responsible for Napoleon's success, so did unity of command eventually result in his downfall:

1. His organization became so large that without a well-organized general staff, it was no longer possible for even a genius to manage it.
2. Napoleon's marshals had not been promoted to command, but rather to obey; therefore he had no skilled "commanders" in his general staff.

3. His enemies recognized their own lack of unity and, refusing to fight independently, organized an alliance.

Clearly someone must be in charge. When everyone decides everything, no one really decides anything. Rule by committee becomes rule by compromise and mediocrity. The inevitable result when decisions are made by "everyone" is that no one is responsible.

Clearly someone must be in charge. Napoleon wrote the general assembly saying, "One bad general is better than two good ones."

Clearly someone must be in charge. The uncanny ability of modern communications to reach into every nook and cranny tends to concentrate all of the power in a single person, who, through overwork, is too often in over his head.

And so it would appear that the extremes of communication—rule by committee and concentration of power—do not work well. There is no one command system that is best for every organization. Command systems radically different from one another have led to equally good results.

Overcentralized management of a marketing organization makes field managers "turn around and face the rear." In overcentralized structures, a manager's success in the organization depends more on how he or she relates to headquarters than to customers. As a result, these managers and the organization lose touch with the market, and disaster follows.

Some solutions require your presence in the field; others require good command systems. If you want to get your marketing close to the customer, empower those who are close to the customer.

ORDERS VERSUS INSTRUCTIONS

Do not issue orders from your ivory tower that must be obeyed exactly. Orders should be issued only when you are present at the scene of action.

When you are not present, then instructions should serve as guidelines. This is usually the better option because it moves decision making closer to the customer.

Beware of the tendency to correct a problem by issuing orders that destroy initiative and freedom of action. Do not create a new rule to cover every circumstance. You can correct an occasional mistake, but you may not be able to win back a lost customer because someone followed orders to the letter.

POWER UP FRONT

The information available to headquarters can never be as accurate or as timely as desired. Fast, accurate, decisive response increases when decisions are made closest to the scene of action.

The concept of power up front, adapted from the Israeli army, gives the field maximum flexibility in all areas except those concerning the selection of objectives. While field commanders may achieve objectives by any means they see fit, they may not change objectives.

The business application we know as empowerment requires clear identification of the boundaries of authority. We have true empowerment when those boundaries are expanded to the maximum. Training ensures the authority is properly used.

Everyone at every level should be conscious that omission and inactivity are far worse than resorting to the wrong expedient.

THE MISSION-ORIENTED COMMAND SYSTEM

With this system, managers tell their people what to do, but not how to do it. Here is how it was originally outlined in the military services:

1. The mission must express the will of the commander in an unmistakable way.
2. The objective, course of action, and constraints on the mission (such as time) must be clear and definite without restricting freedom of action more than necessary in order to make use of the initiative of individuals responsible for getting the task accomplished.
3. Limits as to the method of execution, within the framework of the higher commander's will, are imposed only when essential for coordination with other commanders.

The business translation is simple:

1. Communicate a clear understanding of the mission. That is, establish the purpose and the deliverables.
2. Allow freedom in how to proceed. Do not control the activities necessary to reach the objective.
3. Establish only those rules that are absolutely necessary.

Build
Morale

In order to kill the enemy,
our men must be roused to anger.

To gain enemy's property,
our men must be rewarded
with war trophies.

Bestow rewards irrespective of customary practice and issue orders irrespective of convention and you can command a whole army as though it were but one man.

Accordingly, in chariot battle, when more than ten chariots have been captured, those who took the enemy chariot first should be rewarded.

Then, the enemy's flags and banners should be replaced with ours; the captured chariots mixed with ours and mounted by our men.

—Sun Tzu

It is through kindness that the people are assisted and through duty that they make war.

- *By knowledge matters are decided.*
- *By bravery people fight.*
- *By confidence they are united.*
- *By profit they are stimulated.*
- *By capacity they gain victory.*

"The Precepts of Ssu Ma Jang Chu"
Fourth Century B.C.

168

THE HUMAN SPIRIT CAN BE THE MOST IMPORTANT FACTOR IN SUCCESS, BUT ONLY WHEN RELEASED BY SENIOR COMMANDERS

Morale is a by-product of good management. Although high morale is a component of good management, morale is not a separate objective. High morale happens when leaders do the "right things."

Napoleon believed that "the moral is to the physical as three is to one." That is, moral strength has three times the power of physical strength. In striving for efficiency, we often ignore the overwhelming pressure that this moral force can bring to bear on effectiveness. In business, the moral force can be organized around the belief that we are doing the right thing.

Captain H. M. Johnstone wrote, "Thrice is he armed who has his quarrel just and history shows that the assurance that his god is fighting on his side, and that he is fighting god's quarrel, puts a keen edge on the sword and nerves the arm as nothing else can do."

The doctrine of the Israeli Palmach was that officers should "pull" their men after them by being the first to advance instead of "pushing" their men forward by direct orders. In a withdrawal from a hilltop near Jerusalem, the only way to save at least part of the forces was to leave behind a rear guard that would almost certainly be killed. The command was issued, "All privates will retreat; all commanders will cover their withdrawal."

The business application often takes a different course— golden parachutes are provided to senior officers while the rank and file must fend for themselves. When American Airlines executives asked employees for pay reductions and kept big bonuses for themselves, the employees, whose morale was already low, exploded in anger.

General James H. Merryman, former Army deputy chief of staff, says, "You've got to set a good example. You can't just talk a good line. You can fool your seniors and peers sometimes, but you can't fool the subordinates. There are a thousand little things that only the troops are going to see. After 6 months, they know you—they'll either respect you, and do anything for you or they'll just tolerate you."

Gain Strength from Victory

*The prisoners of war
should be kindly treated and kept.*

*This is called "becoming stronger
in the course of defeating the enemy."*
—Sun Tzu

SEEK COHESION

The Chinese warlords believed that the successful assimilation of the opponent's forces was important. One of Sun Tzu's contemporaries wrote:

"All the soldiers taken must be cared for with magnanimity and sincerity—so they may be used by us."
—Chang Yu

Retention of front-line staff after acquisitions is of special importance to the marketing professional, because these are the people who know the customers—and whom the customers know.

PEOPLE CAUSE ACQUISITIONS TO SUCCEED OR FAIL

The following comments are excerpted from a report by retail guru Robert Kahn, whose observations are based on a military study of the U.S. Army Rangers.

171

Whether the Rangers gained success was strongly influenced by the quality of opposing forces. The quality was
not so much the sum of the abilities of individual
Rangers measured against the sum of enemy skills as it
was the relative cohesion and morale of the forces
engaged. . . . (Significant Ranger victories were won
over enemies who had lost most of their tactical
integrity.)

When the Rangers lost cohesion, they, too, became
less effective. The Rangers' loss of cohesion was less tactical than morale, however, and came about through the
assignment of new men as replacements for casualties.
These new men had not been with the Rangers when
they were first activated, had not gone through training
with the original Rangers, and were not as thoroughly
integrated into the Rangers as those men who had been
with them from the beginning. (The Rangers were
defeated in several battles involving units that had
recently suffered a heavy loss of seasoned troops.)

Kahn analyzed comparable retail situations and found that
many acquired companies disappeared after the acquisition. In
the case of the acquired companies, the new and the old were
not properly integrated—the same problem the Rangers had
with new arrivals who had not trained with the old hands.

Kahn points out that frequent changes of commanding officers did not help the Rangers—nor does it help in business. He
says, "We believe our financial planners too much and our people handlers too little."

Too often the acquisition results in a housecleaning of com-
petent and qualified people. The termination of employees after
acquisitions reduces feelings of loyalty. People realize that
many years of faithful service can go out the window when the
acquisition troops arrive.

Top executives have reason to be concerned when their company is acquired. In larger companies, some 50 percent leave during the first 3 years following acquisition. As might be expected, staff officers leave faster than operating officers

The result is that the acquired company becomes weaker before it becomes stronger—if it survives at all.

Whatever side you are on in an acquisition, marketing should always be most concerned about the effect on the customer.

Back to Basics

*The chances of failure are high
when the rules that ensure victory are ignored.*

There are five points in which victory may be predicted:

1. *He who knows when to fight and when not to fight.*
2. *He who understands how to handle both superior and inferior forces.*
3. *He whose ranks are united in purpose.*
4. *He who is well prepared and lies in wait for an enemy who is not well prepared.*
5. *He whose generals are able and not interfered with by the sovereign.*

It is in these five points that the way to victory is known. Therefore, I say:

Know the enemy and know yourself, and you can fight a hundred battles with no danger of defeat.

When you are ignorant of the enemy but know yourself, your chances of winning and losing are equal.

If ignorant both of your enemy and of yourself, you are sure to be defeated in every battle.

—Sun Tzu

PLAY THE FUNDAMENTALS

National championship football coach at the University of Tennesseee Philip Fulmer gives these basic rules for coaching that can be applied to marketing success:

174

Stress the fundamentals: A team doesn't need to have the best players in order to win if the players are fundamentally sound. A good fundamental football team always blocks and tackles better than its opponents. If you get into trouble, go back to the fundamentals.

Believe in the system: The formation isn't critical as long as you make optimum use of your personnel. The key is to teach the fundamentals within a chosen system and to have everyone believe that the system being used provides the best chance for success.

Be flexible: The adjustments a coach can make depend on how flexible the team is within the system, how much the players know, and how much experience the coaches have.

Know the statistics: "I assumed that we had a 60 to 70 percent chance of success in going for two points after the touchdown because the play starts on the opponent's 3-yard line. When I studied the relevant statistics, I found to my surprise that the national average for success was only 41 percent. When I reviewed our record, I found we had a 44 percent conversion rate. We were only three points better than the national average." This is the kind of data that makes a coach stop and think before he goes for two.

Work from a sound strategy: A coach's strategy should be reflective of his or her personality. Speed and skill levels are key components underlying the development of both offense and defense.

Be prepared: Planning is done long before the game is played. Using a play or formation that has worked in practice is not serendipity, it's planning and preparation.

Organize
for Victory

*Management of a large force
is the same in principle
as the management of a few men:
it is a matter of organization.*

*To direct a large army to fight is the same as to direct a small one: it is
a matter of command signs and signals.*

—Sun Tzu

*"An underadministrated army, however hard and determined, is likely
to run into grave difficulty. . . .*

*An overadministrated army, on the other hand, is prone to defensive mindedness; commanders beset by excessive red tape rarely have
the chance to show originality."*

—David G. Chandler
Atlas of Military Strategy

THE ORGANIZATION EXISTS
SO THAT TASKS CAN BE MANAGED,
PEOPLE SUPPORTED,
AND RESULTS ACHIEVED

The chain of command is not forged with links of even length or
equal strength.

As an army or business grows in size, some organizational
structure becomes necessary. As the organization becomes
divided into line and staff officers, frictions arise. Much of the
problem comes from personal orientation.

176

If the executive's daily life revolves around the corporate headquarters, she or he will see all problems and solutions in relation to the corporate structure. To the extent the executive is in the field, he or she will see problems and solutions in relation to the needs of the market.

Organizations that discourage travel to the field tend to internalize themselves. The marketing plans of these organizations have little chance of success because they are not nourished with current knowledge and a "feel" for the market.

The size of the bureaucracy has a definite impact on speed, and on whether there is any offensive action. The problem is that bureaucratic organizations tend to be defensive. Committees do not take responsibility for actions.

Managers in organizations where the structure is lean must dispense with everything that is not urgent and essential. They must focus on what produces results. In organizations where the structure is fat, managers invent new functions and procedures. The growing complexity of the ever-increasing layers of relationships makes it difficult to focus on the essential.

When the bureaucracy tries to correct itself, it often stumbles over its own rules.

Obviously, the best marketing administrative solution is somewhere between lean and fat. Decentralization that pushes decision making to lower levels is often better than centralization that stifles decision making.

Here are guidelines for decision makers:

1. *Have a plan.* This is the number one problem. You cannot improve without a sense of direction or priorities.
2. *Listen to employees.* Customer research tells you what is happening. Employee research tells you why. Every action to improve involves everyone.
3. *Don't overrely on staff input.* You need line involvement.
4. *Don't ignore middle managers.* They can be a catalyst for implementation.

5. *Respond to problems that surface.* For example, if you do an employee survey, but don't discuss the results and take action, people know that you really don't care.
6. *Invest in training.* If turnover is the source of your reluctance to train, you have a self-fulfilling prophecy.
7. *Invest in recovery.* When you don't solve the customer's problem, you disappoint the customer twice.

Communicate Clearly

As the voice cannot be heard in battle,
gongs and drums are used.

As troops cannot see each other clearly in battle,
flags and banners are used.

The book of Army Management says: "Hence, in night fighting, usually use drums and gongs; in day fighting, banners and flags." Now, these instruments are used to unify the action of the troops.

When the troops can be thus united, the brave cannot advance alone, nor can the cowardly retreat. This is the art of directing large masses of troops.

—Sun Tzu

EMOTIONS CLOUD COMMUNICATIONS

In interpersonal communications, the first rule is to focus on listening to what the other person wants to say. The second rule is to avoid emotional reactions—when that possibility arises, treat the discussion clinically. Business psychologists Rogers and Roethlisberger advise, "This tendency to react to any emotionally meaningful statement by forming an evaluation of it from our own point of view is the major barrier to communications."

IMPLEMENT WAYS TO GET MESSAGES RECEIVED AND UNDERSTOOD

The following mental blocks can impede the flow of information:

The individual's "clarity" threshold: This is the point at which a person sees an event with enough clarity to understand it. When people are confronted with evidence of change, they tend not to take the first input seriously—that is, "one robin does not make a spring."

The three to five rule: It usually takes three to five observations before the input is believed. That is, it takes three to five robins to make a spring. If we do not want spring to come, it may take even more robins.

The preconceived notion: We have definite opinions as to what to expect, and we tend to resist input that is counter to our expectations. For example, the radar operators at Pearl Harbor expected friendly planes and made that assumption. When we plan an event and believe it's going to work, we ignore reports of failure. We assign quality factors to incoming information and will reject the information if the sender is unknown.

The reputation assessment: Our willingness to transmit news depends upon our assessment of the reputation of the messenger and how that news affects our personal reputation. Perhaps, we prefer to "shoot the messenger." Good news travels fast; bad news will be delayed as long as we think the outcome will change.

The act of communication: Before a message can be sent, it must be formed in the mind of the sender. Quantitative values get in the way. Words such as "a lot of customers" or "a variety of lower prices" can have widely different meanings to different people.

We have a need to clarify and quantify information. Our passion for numbers too often means that if something cannot be quantified or measured, it will not be believed. There is no alternative to looking the sender in the eye and hearing the tone of voice.

180

Do Completed Staff Work

*Normally, in war,
the general receives his commands
from the sovereign.*
—Sun Tzu

WORLD WAR II
LETTER OF
INSTRUCTIONS

**WAR DEPARTMENT
HEADQUARTERS ARMY AIR FORCES
WASHINGTON, SEPTEMBER 17, 1942**

ADMINISTRATIVE PRACTICES

COMPLETED STAFF WORK

1. The following exposition of "completed staff work" is published by the headquarters for all members of the staff.

2. This matter is not published as a directive. However, it has great merit, and it is believed that an occasional reading of this treatise and a continual effort to practice this doctrine will be of immense value in building up really good staff work.

3. "Completed staff work" is the study of a problem, and the presentation of a solution, in such a form that all that remains to be done on the part of the head of the division is to indicate his approval or disapproval of

the completed action. The words "completed action" are emphasized because the more difficult the problem is, the more the tendency is to present the problem to the chief in piecemeal fashion. It is your duty as a staff officer to work the details. You should not consult your chief in the determination of those details, no matter how perplexing they may be. You may and should consult other staff officers. The product, whether it involves the pronouncement of a new policy or affects an established one, should be worked out in finished form.

4. The impulse which often comes to an inexperienced staff officer to ask the chief what to do, recurs more often when the problem is difficult. It is accompanied by a feeling of mental frustration. It is so easy to ask the chief what to do, and it appears so easy for him to answer. Resist that impulse. You will succumb to it only if you do not know your job. It is your job to advise your chief what he ought to do, not to ask him what you ought to do. He needs *answers*, not questions. Your job is to study, write, *restudy*, and *rewrite* until you have evolved a single proposed action the best one of all you have considered. Your chief merely approves or disapproves.

5. Do not worry your chief with long explanations and memoranda. Writing a memorandum to your chief does not constitute completed staff work, but writing a memorandum for your chief to send to someone else does. Your views should be placed before him in finished form so that he can make them his views simply by signing his name. In most instances, completed staff work results in a single document prepared for the signature of the chief, without accompanying comment. If the proper result is reached, the chief will recognize

it as one. If he wants comment or explanation, he will ask for it.

6. The theory of completed staff work does not preclude a "rough draft," but the rough draft must not be a half-baked idea. It must be complete in every respect except that it lacks the requisite number of copies and need not be neat. But a rough draft must not be used as an excuse for shifting to the chief the burden of formulating the action. Avoid submittal of hastily prepared inaccurate material lacking concise, specific, workable recommendations.

7. The "completed staff work" theory may result in more work for the staff officer, but it results in more freedom for the chief. This is as it should be. Further it accomplishes two things:

   a. The chief is protected from half-baked ideas, voluminous memoranda, and immature oral presentments.

   b. The staff officer who has a real idea to sell is enabled more readily to find a market.

8. When you have finished your "completed staff work," the final test is this: If you were the chief, would you be willing to sign the paper you have prepared, and stake your professional reputation on it being right?

By command of Lieutenant General ARNOLD:

/s/George E. Stratemeyer
GEORGE E. STRATEMEYER
Major General, U.S. Army
Chief of the Air Staff

Win Battles
and the War

To win battles and capture lands and cities,
but to fail to consolidate these achievements
is ominous
and may be described
as a waste of resources and time.

And, therefore, the enlightened rulers must deliberate upon the plans
to go to battle, and good generals carefully execute them.

—Sun Tzu

The Master Wu said: "'As to the way to attack an enemy and surround
his stronghold. When his strong places have been reduced, his mansion
will be entered, his revenues taken, and his good confiscated.

But his trees must not be cut down nor his houses sold, nor his mil-
let crops taken, nor his animals killed, nor his grain-stores burnt. You
must show no brutality to the people, and if they wish to surrender, you
must allow them to dwell secure.'"

—"Wu Chi on *The* Art of War"
Fourth Century B.C.

INCREASE BOTH HUMAN RESOURCES
AND MATERIAL ASSETS
WITH EACH VICTORY

The author's favorite definition of the marketing process is,
"Marketing is the buying and selling of things with good will at

a profit. If you can have only one, take good will because it is tomorrow's profit."

That definition implies not only making the first sale, but also building a future business relationship that is nurtured with great service and quality. You want to keep customers because

- The lifetime value of a customer is an awesome number. A customer who spends just $20 a week will spend $1000 in a year and $30,000 or more over a lifetime. In some industries, the numbers can be astounding.
- Repeat customers are happy customers who
  - Tend to increase their purchases each year. We like to buy from people whom we know and trust.
  - Recommend your business to others.
  - Step up to more deluxe products that yield a higher margin.
- The cost of acquiring new customers is high, very high.

The first step in keeping customers is finding out why you lose customers. Customers who defect can tell you exactly what parts of the business you must improve. Unlike conventional marketing research, feedback from defecting customers tends to be concrete and specific. Skillful probing can get to the root cause.

Some would argue that you should lose some customers. When that attitude permeates the company, you are headed in the wrong direction. Instead, head in the direction of zero defections—no lost customers. Thinking that "the customer is always right" keeps you from losing customers.

Making the sale and losing the customer is a dreadful, contagious disease.

Eleventh Principle
Personal Leadership

The general is the body.

The companies are the limbs.

The squads are the fingers and thumbs.

War means force and fighting courage,
while the ordering of battle means skill.

"The Precepts of Ssu Ma Jang Chu"
Fourth Century B.C.

STRATEGICALLY
Personal leadership provides vision.

TACTICALLY
Personal leadership builds morale.

It requires the leader's faith in his or her people and their faith in the leader's ability to win.

Personal leadership in command is where art takes over to control the application of science. This does not mean that the principles are ignored, but rather that a successful leader understands how to properly apply the principles.

It has been wisely said that every commander must possess three qualities: A commander must have the mind of a manager, a leader, and a theorist:

The mind of the manager understands administration.
The mind of the leader understands motivation.
The mind of the theorist understands strategy.

The mix of these three qualities of mind varies with the position and task. The basic mindset of the marketing executive should always evolve from the mind of the leader. As managers advance in rank and responsibility, they must strengthen leadership skills even more than they strengthen managerial skills. This strengthening of leadership skills is necessary to meet the demands made on character and intelligence. It is doubtful that most successful executives view themselves as managers; they

188

probably envision themselves as leaders who manage resources in order to lead complex organizations.

Good leadership differs from good management, which is more of an administrative process. Leadership is the ability to create and articulate a vision with such clarity and vigor that others embrace it as their own. The leadership style differs for each individual because it is founded on individual values and applied on the basis of individual knowledge. To shape our own leadership skills, we must build on our existing values and knowledge.

When we talk of "born leaders," we imply that this ability is inherent. Although people can possess an aptitude in certain skills, research indicates that everyone can improve her or his performance and effectiveness through coaching, practice, and training.

Jack Welch sets forth guidelines for good leadership in his book *Straight from the Gut:*

- *Integrity.* Do not have two agendas; there is only one way, the straight way.
- *Setting a tone.* The leader's intensity determines the organization's intensity.
- *Maximizing the organization's intellect.* Be open and spread good.
- *People first, strategy second.* Great strategies need great leaders.
- *Informality.* Make sure everybody counts. Titles do not matter.
- *Self-confidence.* Have the courage to be open. Be comfortable in your own skin.
- *Passion.* Intensity covers sins. Leaders care.
- *Stretch.* Reach for more than you thought possible.
- *Celebrations.* Energize your organization. Make sure teams have fun accomplishing their objectives.
- *Appraisals all the time.* Everyone knows where she or he stands.

In *My American Journey,* Colin Powell offers insight into the role of leadership. He tells how the leaders were trying to figure out how much practice ammunition soldiers had to fire in order to be proficient. To make comparisons between actual firing experience and the use of training devices, they assigned different training times in each mode to three different battalions. Then they took those battalions out on the firing range and gave each the same number of rounds.

The battalions that did the best were those with the best commanders. Says Powell, "Leadership is the art of accomplishing more than the science of management says is possible."

The author observed a similar result in training seminars for quality management. After several divisions in the same company had received the same training, visits were made to the plants.

The level of success depended on the leadership provided by the manager. Only in those organizations where the manager supported the implementation of the training were improvements initiated.

In a study of leadership, three different faces of character were identified. You may have seen some of these characteristics in yourself, because they can depict evolving stages in a person's development.

- *The operator.* This is the person who has a personal agenda and who has no concern for the welfare of others. Common-sense wisdom about operators is that they are looking out for "number one." These people are positive, productive, and interested in becoming successful executives. The inability of operators to look at situations from another perspective leads to their fatal flaw: an inability to internalize another person's perception of them. They can't put themselves in the other person's shoes.
- *The team player.* This person's stock in trade is the connection to others. Unlike the operator, who is most interested

in what others will do for him or her, the team player is highly sensitive to how others feel about him or her. Using baseball metaphors, the operator is a fastball pitcher, whereas the team player can throw curves—that is, use mutual feelings of trust, respect, and affection to exercise leadership. The critical flaw in team players is their inability to gain perspective on connections and loyalties. The team player is a prisoner of the way she or he is viewed by others.

- *The self-defining leader.* This type of leader is defined by a personal commitment to certain internalized values and ideals. He or she will take risks to pursue his or her convictions. The self-defining leader makes personal judgments about his or her worthiness and follows his or her own conscience. We might think of this individual as a person of character.

The self-defining leader does have the goals of the operator and the concern for the views of others that is so dominant in the team player, but she or he keeps these very human impulses in their proper perspective.

Understanding that these are stages in human development is also useful for realizing that different people require different motivations because they are at different stages of development.

Leaders
Listen
and Learn

It is the business of a general to be quiet and thus
ensure depth in deliberation;
impartial and upright,
and thus keep a good management.

Plunder fertile country to supply your army with plentiful food. Pay
attention to the soldiers' well-being and do not fatigue them. Try to
keep them in high spirits and conserve their energy. Keep the army
moving and devise unfathomable plans.

Generally, when invading a hostile territory, the deeper the troops
penetrate, the more cohesive they will be; penetrating only a short way
causes dispersion.

—Sun Tzu

LEADING THE LEADER

A corporate executive writes: "I have discovered in my own
case that the head of business is not a superman, the exclusive
source of wisdom. Ideas will have to come from others as well.
To a great extent these ideas must come from the organization.
The organization must be made to understand that the leader
depends on it for the leadership he or she hopes to give. In
other words, the organization is to lead the leader—who must
always demonstrate that he or she seeks truth rather than
victory."

THE HIGHER THE RANK, THE MORE IMPORTANT IT IS TO LEARN

The first step in acquiring a new company, taking over a new department, or moving into a new position is to ask questions and listen.

One company's rule for new acquisitions is that no operating managers visit the new company for 2 years. Only after limited contacts with top management and finance personnel do the acquiring company's operating managers begin to visit the various operating departments. I know that this rule allows for a smooth transition because I was on the acquired end of this transaction.

The first step in the Japanese entry into any market is learning—followed by entry, takeover, and holding. It has long been forgotten that Toyota's first entry into the American automobile market was the Toyopet—a miserable failure. The Japanese looked on it as a valuable learning experience in achieving a long-range objective.

A corporate executive moving to a leadership position in a new company did nothing but look, listen, and ask questions for 6 weeks. When one of the authors of this book moved from manufacturing to retailing, he spent weeks serving customers in various departments of the retail stores before taking over his new management position.

The leader does not have a monopoly on creativity and should encourage creative expression from his staff. People who have been able to express their ideas feel better for having been given the opportunity to participate. When the ideas have been accepted, the bond to the organization becomes stronger, and implementation is more enthusiastic and sure to succeed.

The creative ideas expressed by the staff, in turn, help contribute to the base of knowledge that will release the leader's own creativity.

Active listening involves asking questions. This keeps you alert and tuned in. It's even better to have a list of questions prepared (in writing) prior to meetings. Where appropriate, taking notes is another way to stay engaged.

Keep a Balanced Leadership

The expediency of advance or withdrawal
in accordance with circumstances
and the fundamental laws of human nature
are matters
that must be studied carefully by a general.
—Sun Tzu

"Now people's qualities have to be sought out from the masses, and this is done by testing their reputation and conduct. Those thus selected will certainly act uprightly. If they try to act thus, but do not, then one must guide them oneself, and if they try and succeed, then one must not forget to employ them accordingly. It may take up to three times to be successful, for such is man's nature, and this may be called method.

In an army when the rules by which it is controlled are in the men themselves, it is called responsibility. When the rules are applied so that the subordinates obey them through fear, it is called law.

In battle, if kindness does not do, then we employ responsibility, and if there is no obedience, then law, and if there is no mutual confidence, then the truth. If the men are sluggish, they must be stimulated. If they are suspicious, this must be corrected. If they do not trust their superiors, then these must improve their conduct."

—"The Precepts of Ssu Ma Jang Chu"
Fourth Century B.C.

195

COMBINE LEADERSHIP STRENGTH WITH MANAGEMENT STRENGTH

Too often, companies are overmanaged and underled. Leadership and management are different functions. One is not necessarily better than the other. Both are needed.

The problem of balancing concern for human resources with the physical tasks is a difficult one. The solution is usually found in the ranking of priorities. Most often, everyone wins when concern for human resources is the first priority.

The ideal leader is characterized as one who combines excellence as a task specialist with an equal flair for the human or heroic aspects of leadership. The ideal leader demonstrates extreme professionalism combined with a warm humanity. He or she understands that it is people rather than techniques that really count.

In *On the Psychology of Military Incompetence*, Norman Dixon points out that humanitarianism in a senior commander contributes to the commander's success in at least two ways:

1. A concern for human resources helps safeguard against unforeseen disasters.
2. Humanitarianism is a prerequisite for high moral and physical health.

The marketing battle, like the military battle, involves a plan and a leader who wants to execute that plan. The manager and the general succeed because they have an idea and they provide the leadership and the command structure for implementing that idea.

Evidence clearly indicates that the effectiveness of forces is far more dependent on the capabilities of officers to lead and inspire than on the equipment these forces might possess. Tactics often do not make the difference in the marketing battle. Commitment and an intense desire to win are the keys to winning.

Jack Welch gives good advice: "Manage tight when you can make a difference. Manage loose when you can't make a difference."

Improve Your Leadership Ability

The general who understands war
is the controller of his people's fate
and the
guarantor of the security of the nation.

This general is the bulwark of the state: If the bulwark is complete at all points, the state will surely be strong. If the bulwark is defective, the state will certainly be weak. Now, there are three ways in which a sovereign can bring misfortune upon his army:

1. *By ordering an advance while ignorant of the fact that the army cannot go forward, or by ordering a retreat while ignorant of the fact that the army cannot fall back. This is described as "hobbling the army."*
2. *By interfering with the army's administration without knowledge of the internal affairs of the army. This causes officers and soldiers to be perplexed.*
3. *By interfering with direction of fighting, while ignorant of the military principle of adaptation to circumstances. This sows doubts and misgivings in the minds of his officers and soldiers.*

If the army is confused and suspicious, neighboring rulers will take advantage of this and cause trouble. This is simply bringing anarchy into the army and flinging victory away.

—Sun Tzu

197

KEEP A COOL HEAD

At First Bull Run, 21 July 1861

Staff officer: *General, the day is going against us.*
Stonewall Jackson: *If you think so, Sir, you had better not say*
anything about it.

The common cause of leadership failure is the crippling effects of anxiety, not lack of intelligence, says Norman Dixon in his extensive study of military incompetence.

CHANGE
ROLES
AS YOU GROW

The effective marketing leader should be capable of ideas at the highest level of abstraction and capable of action at the most mundane levels of detail. However, the mundane must not rule. Senior managers who exercise control over minor details often do so because it gives them a feeling of control—and, of course, makes others wonder about the leader's ability.

It is not that good people are promoted until they reach a level at which they are incompetent, nor is it that these people have been incompetent all along. Rather, it is simply that they have reached a given level of management by functioning in a certain manner, and they continue to function in the same manner regardless of circumstances.

The manager who was promoted because she or he never made a decision and therefore never made a mistake will continue to perform in the same manner at every management level until the visible effects of indecision become intolerable.

The general wisdom is that there is no substitute for an understanding of the industry in which you compete and the gut feeling that comes from years of experience. From this background, great leadership emerges with a strong vision for building the culture to carry the organization forward. The leader communicates his or her beliefs and values and is surrounded by people who share the same goals. As culture changes take place, new behaviors emerge.

Success is derived from a sincere personal commitment to the values the leader wants to implant, along with continued persistence in reinforcing these values. Successful leaders talk about the great amount of time they spend in instilling these important values. A Maytag president who was a member of the founding family told me that he never made a speech without mentioning quality.

Both in war and in business, the operations of Murphy's Law cannot be avoided except at the price of constant vigilance and great effort. As Helmuth von Moltke the Elder wrote, "In war, with its enormous friction, even the mediocre is quite an achievement." A good military commander does not have to be told to post guards. A good business commander does not have to be told to take reasonable security measures. Yet in the long run it is precisely this kind of thing that makes the difference between competence and incompetence, between victory and defeat.

Ninety percent of good command consists of doing things that prevent problems from happening. Good commanders make their luck by stacking the odds in their favor, then spotting and rapidly capitalizing on every opportunity created by their opponent's mistakes.

The Center for Creative Leadership lists the following behavior of successful leaders:

- *Conduct frequent, short, impromptu meetings.* Get out of the office. Gather firsthand knowledge from more than one person.
- *Delegate tasks and develop subordinates.* To delegate is to charge someone with a task without telling that person how to do it.

- *Develop a system for the timely flow of critical information.* Know what you want to know and when you want to know it. Do not resist new information that might change the course of action.
- *Get rid of routine administrative details.* If you are the boss and it does not require your brainpower, delegate it.
- *Force time for reflection.* The leader should be the last person to be overworked.

Keep a Positive Attitude

A whole army may be robbed of its spirit, and its commander deprived of his presence of mind.

At the beginning of a campaign, the spirit of soldiers is keen; after a certain period of time, it declines; and in the later stage, it may be dwindled to nought.

A clever commander, therefore, avoids the enemy when his spirit is keen and attacks him when it is lost. This is the art of attaching importance to moods.

In good order, he awaits a disorderly enemy; in serenity, a clamorous one. This is the art of retaining self-possession.

—Sun Tzu

Napoleon wrote in his *Maxims*:

> "It is exceptional and difficult to find in one man all the qualities necessary for a great general. That which is most desirable, and which instantly sets a man apart, is that his intelligence or talent, are balanced by his character or courage.
>
> If his courage is the greater, a general heedlessly undertakes things beyond his ability.
>
> If on the contrary, his character or courage is less than his intellect, he does not dare carry out his plans."

HAVE FAITH IN YOUR FUTURE

Sun Tzu's "self-possession" has an equivalent in confidence. The attribute of self-confidence can be distilled from a study of masters of the art of leadership:

- Each successful leader believed in his or her people and in their power to rise to the heights of the endeavor to which he or she called them.
- These leaders also believed in a cause that transcended themselves and their own desires or ambitions.

All great achievement has been accomplished by leaders confident of the success of their missions. Lacking such confidence, many leaders require the question to be put through a series of approvals, with the approval process itself deciding the issue. The executive decides without really deciding when he or she becomes too dependent on statistical, cost-accounting, or information-processing systems. The forlorn hope is that out of these systems will come unassailable support for a specific course of action.

The confidence required of the marketing executive is best expressed by Field Marshall Montgomery in his *History of Warfare*, "Many qualities go to make a leader, but two are vital—the ability to make the right decisions, and the courage to act on the decisions. . . . Above all, he must have moral courage, that resolution and determination which will enable him to stand firm when the issues hang in balance."

Shortly after the September 11 attack, New York City mayor Rudolph Giuliani addressed a prayer service at Yankee Stadium, saying, "To those who say our city will never be the same, I say you are right. It *will be better*."

Colin Powell, in his thoughts to live by, says, "Perpetual optimism is a force multiplier."

There are business parallels in the small groups of people who pioneered computers, in countless small-business enterprises, and in corporate turnaround groups. This is where we find the duality of both belief in a cause and belief in people.

Know the "Arts"
of Leadership

Sun Tzu stresses the arts of

- Husbanding one's strength
- Assessing circumstances
- Employing troops

Close to the field of battle, he awaits an enemy coming from afar; at rest, he awaits an exhausted enemy; with well-fed troops, he awaits hungry ones. This is the art of husbanding one's strength.

He refrains from intercepting an enemy whose banners are in perfect order, and desists from attacking an army whose formations are in an impressive array. This is the art of assessing circumstances.

Now, the art of employing troops is that when the enemy occupies high ground, do not confront him uphill, and when his back is resting on hills, do not make a frontal attack. When he pretends to flee, do not pursue. Do not attack soldiers whose temper is keen. Do not swallow a bait offered by the enemy. Do not thwart an enemy who is returning homeward. When you surround an army, leave an outlet free. Do not press a desperate enemy too hard. Such is the method of using troops.

—Sun Tzu

"The Master Wu said: 'In starting military operations there are five things to consider: First, striving after fame; second, striving after profit; third, intensifying feelings of hostility; fourth, stirring up internal disorder; and fifth, causing famine (among the enemy).'"

—"Wu Chi on *The Art of War*"
Fourth Century B.C.

BE PROFESSIONAL; BE HUMAN

In exploring lists of leadership requirements, one could conclude that every desirable human trait is required. However, human traits must be combined with knowledge and experience in both the marketing discipline and the industry.

Napoleon listed 115 contributing qualities in trying to define the essentials of leadership.

Colonel W. J Wood in *Leaders and Battles* describes three personal "arts" that help make intelligence useful in causing effective action:

1. *Imagination.* This is the great mental leap. It is the Greeks with a hollow wooden horse, MacArthur with his surprise attack at Inchon, Wozniak and Jobs with the Apple computer, and Gates with Microsoft software.

2. *Flexibility.* This is the ability to shift mental gears under pressure without confusing the objective. It is Alexander reorganizing his army into light mobile columns to fight guerrillas, the fast-moving infantry of the German blitzkrieg, General Motors developing the Saturn project, and Wal-Mart organizing cross-docking logistics to speed deliveries and reduce costs.

3. *Judgment.* This is the ability to make a sound assessment, decide upon a course of action, and carry out that action. All are attributes that define the greatest military and business captains. To know what one can do on the basis of available means and do it, to know what one cannot do and refrain from doing it, and to distinguish between the two is the very definition of business greatness, as it is of human genius. Former GE executive Jack Welch notes that we rarely regret acting on our judgment of a situation and often regret not acting.

Beware of
Your Blind Spots

The ruin of the army and death of the general
are inevitable results
of these five dangerous faults.
They must be deeply pondered.

There are five dangerous faults which may affect a general:

1. *If reckless, he can be killed;*
2. *If cowardly, captured;*
3. *If quick-tempered, he can be provoked to rage and make a fool of himself;*
4. *If he has too delicate a sense of honor, he is liable to fall into a trap because of an insult;*
5. *If he is of a compassionate nature, he may get bothered and upset.*

These are the five serious faults of a general, ruinous to the conduct of war.

—Sun Tzu

"A general unable to estimate his capabilities or comprehend the arts of expediency and flexibility when faced with the enemy will advance in a stumbling and hesitant manner, looking anxiously first to his right and then to his left, and be unable to produce a plan. Credulous, he will place confidence in unreliable reports, believing at this moment this and another that. As timorous as a fox in advancing and retiring, his groups will be scattered about. What is the difference between this and driving innocent people into boiling water or fire? Is this not exactly like driving cows and sheep to feed wolves or tigers."

—Tu Mu
Seventh Century, B.C.

FLAWS IN THE PERSONAL CHARACTER
OF THE COMMANDER
WILL CAUSE OPPORTUNITIES
TO BE LOST

Examine carefully these characteristics of incompetence:

- An underestimation, sometimes bordering on the arrogant, of the opponent. ("Those guys are dumb.")
- An inability to profit from past experience. ("Let's do it the same way again.")
- A resistance to adopting and exploiting available technology and novel tactics. ("We tried that before.")
- An aversion to reconnaissance, coupled with a dislike of intelligence—both kinds. (Doesn't do informal or formal research; rejects ideas from people who learn from it.)
- Great physical bravery but little moral courage. (The physical is personal; the moral is in relationships with others.)
- Either imperviousness to suffering or an irrational and incapacitating state of compassion. (That is, either doesn't care or cares too much.)
- Passivity and indecisiveness in dealing with senior commanders. (You can't get an answer or a decision.)
- A tendency to lay blame on others. ("It's the fault of. . . .")
- A love of the frontal assault. ("Let's hit 'em head on.")
- A high regard for tradition. ("The way we've always done it is. . . .")
- A lack of creativity, improvisation, inventiveness, and open-mindedness. (Ideas are met with requests for busy work.)
- Procrastination. ("Let's think about it some more.")

Source: Norman Dixon, *On the Psychology of Military Incompetence.*

The Role of Discipline

The smooth implementation of orders reflects harmonious relationship between the commander and his troops.

If troops are punished before they have grown attached to you, they will be disobedient. If not obedient, it is difficult to employ them. If troops have become attached to you, but discipline is not enforced, you cannot employ them either. Thus, soldiers must be treated in the first instance with humanity, but kept under control by iron discipline. In this way, the allegiance of soldiers is assured.

If orders are consistently carried out and the troops are strictly supervised, they will be obedient. If orders are never carried out, they will be disobedient.

—Sun Tzu

"Alexander's phalanx and Caesar's legions beat hordes of enemies, not because their equipment was better, but because their training and discipline was far superior."

— Col. John G. Burr
The Framework of Battle

DISCIPLINE YOUR MANAGEMENT STYLE

This is not the discipline of "following orders or else," but rather the discipline of following the rules of business success and doing what is right.

Discipline involves

- Setting priorities for action
- Setting standards for performance
- Providing training and coaching to meet the standards

Priorities: There are a lot of things that are nice to do, but only a few that are critical. Determine priorities for self-improvement and for marketing improvement.

Standards: Establishing standards can keep you from playing favorites and being criticized for it. Even more important is that standards set the bar for performance. Standards embody the discipline that takes you to marketing excellence.

Training and coaching: When Management by Objectives was introduced as a management tool, the idea was that the manager and the employee would agree on what was to be done, and the employee would then get it done. It didn't last as a management methodology because the training and coaching phase was missing.

A national championship college basketball coach tells about how she took her team to a workshop at a professional team to learn about the system used by a troublesome competitor. The discipline of standards and priorities was not enough; the coach and the team needed to know what to do and engage in the discipline of practicing how to do it.

Championship athletes have practice disciplines; noted musicians have practice disciplines; why should we think that all of our marketing can be practiced on the championship court? Why do we devote so little time to the discipline of training ourselves and our staff? Only through interactive instruction do we learn the disciplines that lead to good business practices.

ELEVENTH PRINCIPLE

Avoid the Road to Defeat

Six situations cause an army to fail. . . .
When any of these six situations exists,
the army is on the road to defeat.

There are six situations that cause an army to fail. They are: flight,
insubordination, fall, collapse, disorganization, and rout. None of these
disasters can be attributed to natural and geographical causes, but to the
fault of the general.

Terrain conditions being equal, if a force attacks one ten times its
size, the result is flight.

When the soldiers are strong and officers weak, the army is insubordinate.

When the officers are valiant and the soldiers ineffective, the army
will fall.

When the higher officers are angry and insubordinate, and on
encountering the enemy rush to battle on their own account from a feeling of resentment and the commander-in-chief is ignorant of their abilities, the result is collapse.

When the general is incompetent and has little authority, when his
troops are mismanaged, when the relationship between the officers and
men is strained, and when the troop formations are slovenly, the result
is disorganization.

When a general unable to estimate the enemy's strength uses a
small force to engage a larger one or weak troops to strike the strong,
or fails to select shock troops for the van, the result is riot.

When any of these six situations exists, the army is on the road to
defeat. It is the highest responsibility of the general that he examines
them carefully.

—Sun Tzu

FOCUS ON WHAT THE
CUSTOMER WANTS
AND NEEDS

To succeed, the marketing professional needs to actively pursue excellence in the following areas:

1. *Get the marketing decision made before the financial decision.* Come to terms with the financial decision makers. We must serve the customer before we can serve the bottom line.
2. *Be an expert on what the customer thinks, wants, needs, and will purchase.* Demonstrate your professionalism with respect to marketing information. Come to terms with information technology. Take full advantage of the resources available from information systems.
3. *Build a customer-driven culture.* Play an active role in increasing the quality of both the product and the delivery system to the customer. Tear down the functional silos, including the one labeled marketing. Organize everyone to serve the customer.
4. *Think strategically.* Future organizations will be constructed to fit the way customers want to buy, not along product lines, geography, or function. Focus on your customer and your customer's customer. You strategy must carry you to future products and services. Think recycling, new sources of power, the environment, and more.
5. *Think of customers as people.* There are no mass markets. Micromarkets are disappearing. The new "particle market" is one family or one person. Even the term *family* is difficult to define, because there is such a diversity of family structures.
6. *Do not aggravate your customers.* How can you charge a penalty or nuisance fee and still keep the customer? Southwest in air travel and Schwab in financial services succeed with structures that have a minimal level of aggravating nuisance charges.

Earn Loyalty

---

*If a general regards his men as infants,
then they will march with him
into the deepest valleys.*

*He treats them as his own beloved sons
and they will stand by him unto death. . . .*

*If, however, a general is indulgent towards his men but cannot employ
them, cherishes them but cannot command them or inflict punishment
on them when they violate the regulations, then they may be compared
to spoiled children, and are useless for any practical purpose.*

—Sun Tzu

*"The Maruis of Wu enquired saying, 'What is it that makes soldiers
win victories?'*

*Chi replied, 'It is discipline that makes them victorious. . . . What
is meant by discipline is to have ceremony when at rest and stern
menace when in action. . . . It is what is called a father and son
relationship.'"*

—"Wu Chi on *The Art of War*"
Fourth Century, B.C.

DEVELOP A CULTURE
OF INTEGRITY
AND SERVICE

There are two dimensions of loyalty that are important to the
marketing executive: internal loyalty and customer loyalty.

Internal Loyalty

Earning the loyalty of the people you work with and of your peers is pretty simple stuff. It starts with your integrity and whether or not you care. Loyalty is nurtured by an attitude focused on catching people doing things right—or even almost right. Encourage good performance and you'll get more good performance that eventually turns into good business habits—and wins loyalty.

Loyalty is born in the respect that comes from confidence. Loyalty is not something you request. It comes from within the soul of people with whom you have trained and worked and inspired to greater achievements. Hire people who are better than you and inspire them to be loyal, and you will have an organization of giants.

Customer Loyalty

The most visible examples of customer loyalty programs have been in the travel industry. Loyalty programs in the airline industry have been deteriorating, and so has customer loyalty.

There are more miles waiting to be redeemed than most travel providers want to admit. A senior hotel executive who was on the team that instituted a rewards program for his company told me that the team had no idea how many points to award for a night's stay. Many of the decisions were based on matching what competitors were doing.

I like to do business with organizations where

I am greeted by name.
I do not don't have to wait in line.
I am not assessed penalties when I screw up.

These three customer service items represent big opportunities for marketing because getting and keeping customers is a marketing task. The solution is not in training but in fixing the culture of the organization from the top down. Culture is the way we think, work, and act. Culture defines what is permissible and not permissible. Culture advises what can be done for the customer and what cannot be done for the customer.

You have a good culture when turnover is low and the person you know stays with the organization. Then, the opportunity for a business relationship exists. We buy from people whom we know and trust.

Twelfth Principle
Simplicity

Everything is very simple in war.
but the simplest thing is very difficult.

—Carl von Clausewitz
On War

Even the simplest plans are difficult to execute.

Uncomplicated plans clearly expressed promote intelligent understanding.

The mission for Overlord, the Normandy invasion during World War II, which was the largest amphibious operation ever undertaken, was defined on a single page. Although this enormously complex operation was supported by a vast number of detailed orders and schedules, the essence of the plan was quite simple.

The culture at Procter & Gamble teaches presenting your plans on a single page.

Among professionals who do a lot of public speaking, this one-liner tells it all: "I'm sorry this speech was so long, but I didn't have time to prepare."

Simple marketing plans, messages, and ideas communicate best. The ever-elusive Murphy has a few simple, but useful laws:

- If it looks stupid, but works, it isn't stupid.
- No plan survives the first contact intact.
- The important things are always simple.
- The simple things are always hard.

Regarding advertising, the renowned David Ogilvy said, "Keep your opening paragraph down to 11 words." That's the *paragraph* you keep down to 11 words, not the sentence. Billboard experts advise that 14 words is the maximum. You want the reader to get the message. If there are too many words, the message is missed because nothing is read. In advertising, it is often true that the more information you cram into an ad, the less comes out.

We communicate best with simple messages, such as

- Features don't sell, benefits do.
- Get out where the rubber meets the road.
- Managers must walk the talk.

Implementing Strategies

Practical Marketing Examples from Successful Managers

MARKETING ALZHEIMER'S

Calvin L. Hodock
Professor of Marketing *Berkeley College*

In both marketing and warfare, "know thy enemy" is a valuable mantra. Sun Tzu's best-known aphorism on intelligence applies: *Know thy enemy and know thyself. If ignorant both of your enemy and yourself, you are certain in every battle to be in peril.*

The people who are responsible for the new product efforts at many of our blue-chip consumer goods companies should heed the sage counsel of Sun Tzu. It could help to reduce the failure rate of new products. Nine out of ten new products fail at these companies. The wisdom of Sun Tzu could help stamp out Marketing Alzheimer's—a serious malady in innovation malpractice. Many flawed new products are simply carbon copies of ideas that have floundered in the past.

Listerine toothpaste is a good example. It failed twice, both because it had a bad taste and because of negative imagery from its mouthwash heritage. Taste is an important driver in the toothpaste category. Why did Listerine not know this? Marketing Alzheimer's. It is everywhere, like the Visa card.

The beer barons are gluttons for punishment. Desperate for growth, they have chased such ill-fated new products as low-alcohol beer, no-alcohol beer, dry beer, and ice beer. Marketing Alzheimer's strikes again. The marketers from sudsville are now watching their romance with malternatives crash into a fiery ball of flames. Those who forget their history are condemned to repeat it. The precedent for failure was established with the earlier demise of Zima from Coors. Each later attempt has been a victim of history lessons forgotten.

Now the brewers are trying to cash in on health-conscious drinkers with low-carbohydrate beer. Are the beer bellies at the corner pub—the heavy beer drinkers—really concerned about carbs as they hoist a brewskie and munch on an artery-clogging cheeseburger? These low-carb beers are slightly lower in calories than the light beers. Is this a solution to a problem that America doesn't have? History is about to repeat itself as low-carb-beers follow the same path as malternatives, dry beer, and wine coolers—down the tube.

Marketing Alzheimer's has invaded the land of the cola connoisseurs. Coke is trying Cherry Coke for the second time. Both Coke and Pepsi are attempting to market lemon-flavored colas, which have failed before. Why should they succeed this time around? These new products are attempts to energize a cola segment that is fraying at the edges.

In early 1999, Kellogg's introduced Ensemble, a line of psyllium- and oat-based products—pastas, cookies, snack cakes, potato snacks, frozen entrees, and cereals. These are healthy foods that are designed to lower cholesterol levels. Other marketers have tried the line concept before. It never works. History repeats itself, and Kellogg's flunks the history exam.

When dealing with a unified line, supermarkets prefer to scatter the individual products in the appropriate departments around the store. It is impossible to build brand identity for the line with the trade cherry-picking the items in the line. The real estate in stores is too valuable to give any unified line critical mass. Kellogg's should have known this, given the past debacles associated with attempts to sell a line of products in supermarkets.

Here is another mistake from past history that the architects of Ensemble disregarded. Healthy foods geared toward lowering cholesterol levels have been tried before—for example, Intelligent Cuisine from Campbell's Soup. The majority of Americans are clueless about their cholesterol levels. The answers are not in the stars; they can be found in the filing cabinets of history. Neither Intelligent Cuisine nor Ensemble had a sea-change impact on the marketing fortunes of these companies, which were desperate for sales volume given the decline of condensed soup and ready-to-eat cereals.

Sun Tzu says, "Wise generals win because they have fore-knowledge."

The same innovation mistakes are continually repeated, because there is no historical perspective. Why waste resources on new products that have failed before? Establish a knowledge based on innovation. Make new product managers pore through it to improve their innovation IQs.

It might be helpful if the chief marketing officers did the same thing. They would be better prepared the next time they listened to the latest innovation fairy tales from the troops in the trenches.

CUSTOM MARKETING

Bill Malkes
Chief Executive Officer, *Siligence*

In customizing a product or service, the boundaries between marketing (strategy) and selling (tactics) are blurred.

I have encountered unique forms of customized marketing during 20 years of raising venture capital (talk about a cold audience), mergers, acquisitions, joint ventures, and marketing computer circuits.

The industry failure rate for designing complete Systems on a Chip (SoC) is very high. Our success rate has been a satisfying 98 percent. Some of this success can be attributed to integrating the design activities into the sales interface—that is, taking the marketing functions to the sales process.

Recently, I was asked to advise a group of technical support engineers on how they could be more effective in helping to market complex integrated-design chips. My source for structure was the timeless wisdom of Sun Tzu.

Our starting point in the training discussion was the position of support personnel in the customer interface. Sun Tzu said, "It is the business of the general to be quiet and thus assure depth in deliberation."

For some reason, normally reticent engineers become overly talkative in front of a prospect. They cannot refrain from showing the customer how smart they are by reciting everything they know about what they *think* the subject is. Like the general who must deliberate, our support people need to position themselves as listeners and ask questions. As author Gerald Michaelson would say, the more questions you ask, the smarter you get.

This listening strategy works all the way through custom marketing and selling. When I was a young CFO, I had been quite thorough in my preparation of an aggressive marketing program to be presented to the board of directors. I had a beautifully prepared report, complete with risk analysis, graphs, and compelling arguments. The strategy was done; now came the tactics of selling the program to the board of directors. Less than 2 minutes into my presentation, the directors called for a vote and unanimously approved my request. After thanking them, I said, "And another good thing about this is. . . ." I was immediately interrupted by a director, who delivered advice that would last a lifetime: "Bill, nothing good can happen to you by talking now. When you get a yes, stop." The key message for any business executive is "shut up" once you get the order.

Sun Tzu's lesson of being quiet was burned into my subconscious thought in perpetuity. In a less fortunate situation, we employed a salesperson who, in her jubilation at receiving a customer yes on a proposal, said, "And the great thing is that we are giving a 25 percent discount on that product now." Her "career" continued for about 90 days. Listen!

So you listen, but you ask, "Don't we have to talk sooner or later?" Sun Tzu said, "When encamping, select high ground facing the sunny side." Our company takes the high ground by establishing our factors of differentiation. We find the places where we can look down on our competition from the high ground of competitive advantage.

It is time for my personal favorite wisdom from the master: "Use the normal force to engage; the extraordinary to win." The most successful salespeople in our organization have grown by knowing the skills of individual design centers. Then they go the extra mile by getting the engineers in those centers in front of customers who need their particular skill. The salespeople who are victorious know not only what the customer wants, but also his or her fears and the source of those fears. We win by letting the customer gain confidence through an interface with the design engineers. It is analogous to having the tech-savvy television customer talk to the marketing and production personnel. Our marketing support people now know whether the prospect wants dinner at a five-star restaurant or dinner at a greasy spoon and a football game. They know how to design to the customer's specifications. They know how to leverage the extraordinary.

"Conformation of the ground is of great assistance in military operations." The design of a complex System on a Chip can take more than a year and cost well over a million dollars, with no guarantee of success. It is a risky proposition. Knowing the customer's business model (confirming the ground) is of utmost importance. We maximize the customer's profit in terms of 5-year projections and minimize our engineering costs in terms of weekly amounts, or even daily amounts. Somewhere between long-term profits and daily costs, the process can get appreciably less risky.

Finally, we talked about the principle of maneuver—thinking on your feet. Said Sun Tzu, "Tactics change in an infinite variety of ways to suit changes in the circumstances."

The biggest and most profitable customer booked during my tenure actually had given a verbal purchase order to its existing design firm. How did we win? We were acquired by an organization that increased our skill sets, and so we were now technically competitive. An alert saleswoman changed her tactics when she heard of the acquisition and put our team in front of the customer.

Another problem arose: The competitive design house had access to the industry's "Goliath," which had a component that was integral to the proposed design. Our team could not provide the component, so we changed the battlefield. We called on a relationship with the industry "David" and demonstrated that David was a winning fit.

A lot can happen on a 16-month project. Halfway through the project, one of our key partners could not meet one of the customer's requirements. The vendor's failure was announced in the trade press, and the customer knew about it. We adjusted our tactics and found a new partner that we believed was the only company that could meet the tough requirement. The solution was presented to the customer, and for the third time we "won the job."

For many years I have benefited from the guidance of Sun Tzu and Michaelson's interpretations. It has served well. New business quotes and customer calls are up subsequent to our custom-marketing conference, and our support engineers are involved in the selling process like never before.

WISE LESSONS

Jeff Tripician
Managing Partner, *TM branding*

It seemed like an obvious opening line for a speech at the Dairy Industry's annual meeting in Chicago. The audience consisted of approximately 2000 dairy executives from over 500 firms that made up almost 100 percent of the milk industry in the United States. As the new 32-year-old vice president of sales and marketing for the industry, charged with developing the business strategies and tactics required to turn around the sagging milk business, I was confident that this was the correct stage to show all those in attendance the quality of the thinking that they would see over the coming years.

My opening line was, "Milk as a beverage does not compete well with the Cokes and Pepsis of the world, and therefore we must change if we are to be successful."

The format of the conference allowed for roving microphones, and less than 15 seconds into my hour-long speech, a very elderly gentleman in the front row flagged down a roving microphone and stood to speak.

Slightly annoyed, I stopped my speech and motioned for the man to ask his question. I thought that possibly the PA system was not working or the slides were out of focus.

Unfortunately, I was wrong on both counts. The gentleman simply stated, "Young man, I have been in this industry since before you were born, and my family for three generations before that, so let me enlighten you: Milk is *not* a beverage."

And with that simple statement, this innocent-looking 80-year-old gutted my speech and sent me to the corner of the room with a dunce cap on my head.

This was not the way it was supposed to be. I had researched the beverage industry exhaustively over the prior months, preparing for this first encounter with the milk industry leadership. This was the eve of the vote to fund the industry's multi-year program to rebuild Milk. And I was the hotshot who had been anointed to "fix the mess" that had been created by over 30 years of marketing neglect by these same people.

Fortunately for me, another elderly gentleman, a senior statesman of the industry and CEO of one of the largest dairies in the country, rose from the middle of the room and addressed the room. "I did not come to Chicago to listen to the same tired old ideas that we have debated for years," he said. "I came here to listen to and support new thinking. I do not know if the plan we are about to hear and vote on will work, but I do know that our old plans and thinking have failed us."

With that, I was back on track, and the speech was a big hit and the vote a success. I was also armed with two new pieces of knowledge: First, have a healthier appreciation for the troops, and second, hold all questions until the end of the speech.

Upon my return to my office in Washington, my CEO (a wise and battle-scarred veteran of the dairy industry for over 35 years) sat me down in his sitting room/library to discuss the meeting. Behind me was a wall of books and signed pictures from dignitaries, all very impressive.

The CEO started with, "You're a hell of a smart marketer, but you have a lot to learn about leadership." This began my 4-year postgraduate education on Sun Tzu at the hands of one of his most ardent students, my CEO.

Lesson 1: *"If You Know Yourself, but Not the Enemy, for Every Victory Gained, You Will Suffer Defeat"*

While the people in my own industry were not the enemy, they were hostile. My understanding of the beverage industry had not prepared me properly to marshal the troops. I did not have their hearts and minds. I spent the next 6 weeks traveling the country, visiting dairies one on one, listening to their issues, and incorporating them into my own ideas for winning this beverage war.

Lesson 2: *"Use Many to Strike the Few"*

During my travels, I discovered a small but vocal group of industry leaders who shared my vision for the future. These individuals formed the backbone of my advisory staff and led five industry teams that shaped and recommended action plans for the entire industry. Appointing members from their own ranks and having them recommend action proved to be a superior strategy for uniting the industry behind bold thinking—its own bold thinking.

Lesson 3: *"When the Troops Are United, the Brave Cannot Advance Alone, nor Can the Cowardly Retreat"*

My travels also revealed unique insights into the industry that, when turned into battlefield tactics, acted to unite the industry. As you might imagine, an industry composed largely of family-owned dairies was not willing to turn over its future to some centralized semigovernmental group in Washington, D.C. These dairies needed to be able to roll up their sleeves and fight for their business. As a result, all the programming that we developed had two components: a national effort and a localized effort that was run by them. This strategy forced them to act as one, independent yet interdependent units.

Lesson 4: *"All Armies Prefer High Ground to Low"*

In hindsight, starting the speech by pointing out our weakness and our failure simply angered the crowd. A better strategy would have been to speak of our unique successes, our positives ("the high ground"), and how we could utilize them to prosecute the war to a successful conclusion.

I should have referred to those aspects of the product that were positive and with which the group was comfortable, such as "trust, quality, wholesomeness, freshness, and nutrition," as the cornerstones of our future success. This would have been a rallying cry that everyone in the room could have supported.

I learned from and applied this lesson, and as the program developed over the years, we crafted all our messages around these positive cornerstones that the industry embraced and took to market as *its message*.

Lesson 5: *"The Law of Successful Operations Is to Avoid the Enemy's Strength and Strike Weakness"*

In focusing on and leveraging the milk industry's inherent strengths of "trust, freshness, quality, wholesomeness, and nutrition," not only did we solidify support within our own ranks, but we attacked the competition in its areas of greatest weakness. Coke and Pepsi could ill afford to attack milk on any of the five fronts that formed the core of our consumer communication.

Lesson 6: *"The Possibility of Victory Lies in the Attack"*

This was the most enduring lesson learned by the staff, the agencies, the dairies, and myself. For years, the milk industry had stood for the same five communication points just outlined, but it had done little to communicate them or reinforce them with consumers. It was only after we collectively focused our energies in a coordinated and disciplined attack on those that were eroding our position that the industry won back valuable consumer and retailer real estate.

This proactive and focused attack that targeted our enemy's inherent weakness produced results far ahead of expectation.

Four years and countless "meetings" with the CEO taught me that despite all the technological advances, all the studies on human behavior, and the advent of "instant everything," the true keys to success and failure both on the battlefield and in the boardroom have not changed since a Chinese general first identified them over 2500 years ago.

OFFENSIVE STRATEGY

Art Saxby
Vice President, Marketing, *Imperial Sugar Company*

Therefore I say: Know the enemy and know yourself; in a hundred battles you will never be in peril.

When you are ignorant of the enemy but know yourself, your chances of winning or losing are equal.

If ignorant both of your enemy and of yourself, you are certain in every battle to be in peril.

A number of years ago, I was an analyst in the strategic planning group at a snack food producer. The company had a number of very tough regional competitors. Our objective was not only to be a strong brand in every market but to be the most profitable. With twin objectives of profit and market share, we knew that we could not throw our weight around and drive prices down just to win share. That would have weakened the target competitors more than it weakened us, but it would also have driven the profitability right out of the market.

Before formulating an attack plan, we turned an eye inward and analyzed ourselves. We looked at our own profitability in the target market in detail. We not only analyzed the profitability of each brand, size, and sales channel, but also looked at the key factors that could cause changes in that profitability. In doing this analysis, we ignored the internal financial reports. Instead, we built a view of the cost structure as if we were on the outside looking in. We looked at the types of equipment installed and the crewing and labor rates. Then, from public market-share data, we determined average production run times, number of package size or flavor changeovers a week, and so on.

Once this was complete, we compared the information to the internal cost and production efficiency reports. This gave us confidence in two key areas. First, we now knew the specific areas of our business that were driving our profitability and the specific types of market actions that would have the most or least impact on that profitability. In other words, prior to starting hostilities, we knew what areas we needed to defend and the specific types of counterattacks that would be the most damaging. Second, we were confident that we could apply the same methodology to our competitors.

The second phase of the project was to gather information about our competitors. Our internal study had shown us the key information to look for. We looked through public building permits and trade journals to determine the types of equipment our competitors had installed. We looked at public EPA records to evaluate raw material efficiencies, and we performed time studies to determine our competitors' average sales and distribution efficiency.

Once we had compiled all of this information, we could truthfully say that we knew the enemy as well as we knew ourselves. From this, several interesting things came to light. Most important, the competitors' high-volume items in the high-volume supermarket channel were delivering them very little profit. These items covered a lot of fixed costs, but they delivered almost no profit. If we had gone with our first instinct—hit the competitors' big guns with our big guns in the biggest sales channel—we would have found ourselves standing toe to toe slugging it out, but never really accomplishing anything. This would have been akin to Sun Tzu's comments: "The worst policy is to attack cities. Attack cities only when there is no alternative."

Our analysis also showed that while the large brands sold in the high-volume supermarket channel generated almost no profit, the small brands of certain snack foods sold to small convenience stores, gas stations, and delis generated all of the company's profits.

This information aided us in organizing a strong offense and defense that increased our market share and profits.

SEIZING THE HIGH GROUND

Randy Gray
Vice President and General Manager,
Brunswick Boat Group

Over the past few decades, I have witnessed extraordinary performance from a select group of companies that appear to follow Sun Tzu's principle that both in battle and in maneuvering, all armies prefer the high ground. Each of us could make his or her own list of high-performance companies, but I would submit that most of us would find it difficult to omit such names as General Electric, Microsoft, Intel, Nike, Coke, Wal-Mart, and Toyota/Lexus. While I do not profess to understand the strategic plans of each of these leading companies, one can generalize that all of these firms use techniques in their business strategy and marketing initiatives that generally follow the principles of Sun Tzu in their focus on winning the war, not the battle.

During my career, I have spent a great deal of time studying and developing strategies to gain competitive advantage in various fields, from teaching to managing domestic and international businesses. While there is no simple cookbook recipe that will ensure success, I have observed that there does tend to be a set of characteristics that are generally common to highly successful companies. Winning companies tend to have one or more of the following attributes: (1) best cost position, (2) leadership in employing innovation/technology, (3) strong brand position, (4) highly efficient distribution, and/or (5) superior customer service.

Low costs may be the ultimate competitive weapon, and nearly all the companies listed here have been successful in delivering superior margin performance in their industries by paying close attention to costs. In today's challenging environment, it is vitally important to achieve superior margin performance in

233

order to effectively follow Sun Tzu's philosophy of seizing the high ground to build superior mass (e.g., GE's dedication to being number one or a strong number two in each of its businesses). Superior mass is an essential Sun Tzu principle if one believes the doctrine that *a weak force will eventually fall to a stronger one*. I have found that when you find your market position being vigorously attacked in business, having mass and the best cost position is a great defense.

Intel and Microsoft are excellent examples of companies that not only have achieved the high ground but have followed Sun Tzu's principle of consolidating their position by leveraging speed in technology and innovation to sustain strategic advantage. Sun Tzu notes that "speed is of the essence in war and what is valued is a quick victory." Certainly, Intel's successful pursuit of Moore's law of power in chips and Bill Gates's aggressive new product launches with enhanced performance at Microsoft have provided powerful examples of how speed in innovation and technology in the development of new products can deliver sustained success.

The power of brand continues to be a great differentiator in the success of companies. Nike and Coke have developed unmatched brand positions in their industries by doing extraordinary marketing. Sun Tzu states, "Those skilled in war can make themselves invincible. Know the weather and know the ground and victory will be complete." Nike and Coke have surely followed the rule of knowing themselves, their customers, and their enemies and, as a result, have established nearly unassailable positions. It is surely possible to copy a cola or a pair of sneakers, but it is not possible to copy the power of the brand. Several years ago, I had the opportunity in the marine business to leverage in-depth knowledge of the customer with the power of the brand to thwart an attack by a powerful competitor. I would recommend that the business strategist never underestimate the power of this combination.

The skill of Sam Walton and his successor organization in managing costs and efficient distribution at Wal-Mart is legendary. In a relatively short period of time, Wal-Mart has dethroned one leading retailer after another to become the world's largest company. Wal-Mart appears to be an excellent example of Sun Tzu's principle of *concentrating effort where one has strength*. The power of the most efficient distribution combined with a relentless focus on achieving the lowest costs has enabled Wal-Mart to double sales per square foot over the past 5 years, despite its massive size. Perhaps another of Sun Tzu's principles is equally evident in the Wal-Mart philosophy, as it appears that Wal-Mart recognizes that *management of a large force is the same in principle as management of a few men; it is a matter of organization.*

Seeking to challenge Mercedes for the leadership position in the luxury vehicle market, Toyota used Sun Tzu's principle of knowing yourself and knowing the enemy by combining superb product expertise with superior customer service when introducing Lexus. The results have been remarkable, as recent J D Power surveys have consistently showed Lexus ahead of Mercedes in customer satisfaction. Clearly, Lexus strategists used the power of information to focus resources to create a novel customer experience by eliminating the hassle in luxury automobile ownership.

As vice president and general manager of a customer-focused parts and accessories business, eliminating hassle for our current and future customers is my overarching goal.

Index

INDEX